Witchcraft

Witchcraft
By Walter B. Gibson

GROSSET & DUNLAP
A NATIONAL GENERAL COMPANY

Publishers   New York

COPYRIGHT © 1973 BY WALTER B. GIBSON
ALL RIGHTS RESERVED

LIBRARY OF CONGRESS CATALOG CARD NUMBER: 72-156327
ISBN: 0-448-02182-X

PUBLISHED SIMULTANEOUSLY IN CANADA

Second printing

PRINTED IN THE UNITED STATES OF AMERICA

Contents

1. Witchcraft Among the Ancients.................. 1
2. The Druids and Their Legends.................. 8
3. Witchcraft Comes of Age...................... 18
4. The Devil's Disciple........................... 29
5. Witchcraft on the Wing....................... 36
6. The Hammer of the Witches................... 43
7. The Call Goes Out............................ 54
8. Skeptics Versus Believers...................... 64
9. The Witch Finders and Their Ways............. 72
10. Vampires: Devils in Human Form.............. 78
11. The Kiss of Death............................ 85
12. Lycanthropy: Werewolves and Their Kin........ 96
13. The Power of the Hex........................ 107
14. Africa: Home of Witchcraft................... 116
15. Voodoo and Modern Devil Worship............ 126
16. Witchcraft Today ... and Tomorrow........... 138

Witchcraft

1
Witchcraft Among the Ancients

Witchcraft has been classed properly as the world's oldest profession. Among the Australian aborigines, who are the earth's most primitive people, the only professional class is the witch doctor, who reputedly can kill victims at a distance or bring back a victim from the brink of death by counteracting the evil efforts of a fellow member of the craft.

Similar powers have been claimed by witches and their kind in every land in every period, and the scope and complexity of the powers of witches have increased as man has attained higher levels of civilization. But the basic pattern is the same and the potential — often solely for evil — is as great whether the practitioner is an ignorant native squatting in the Australian bush or the "god" of a modern witch coven disporting in a luxurious "temple" laden with the smoke of exotic incense and buoyed up by LSD.

Among the services performed by the primitive Australian wizard is that of placing a stone in the fork of a tree to hold up the setting sun long enough for hunters to return home before dark. African witch doctors do exactly the same for a traveler starting out in the morning, prolonging his day, at least in his imagination. Australian witch doctors, working in concert, are said to make or break storms, either bringing rain or diverting damaging winds, as the situation may demand; and the same power was long attributed to English witches, though always with ill intent.

Australian bushmen have even sworn that they have seen those same witch doctors riding the clouds they have summoned, which is not surprising, since European peasants long insisted that they often spotted local witches skimming along the crests of hailstorms and even claimed to have brought some down with gunfire.

While witchcraft was well-known throughout the ancient world, it really hit its stride among the Romans, and it is from their period that much of modern witchery is derived. There are three outstanding reasons for this: First, the Romans inherited a strong brand of witchcraft from the Etruscans, who inhabited Italy before them. Next, the Romans were great borrowers from other religions; whenever they conquered a nation, they felt free to take over its gods as well as its government, and that included witch lore. Finally, as the empire spread, the Romans superimposed their traditions upon those of other lands.

Peculiar to the Romans were the Lares and Penates, household gods that protected hearth and home; though there were Lares and Penates that belonged to the state as well. In addition, the Romans worshipped the Manes, spirits of their ancestors, who supposedly dwelt deep below the earth and emerged through sacred pits on special days. Through witchcraft, the Manes could be raised as ghosts, but they could also appear in dreams to give warnings of their own accord.

Sibyl, the witch of legend who lived to an age of a thousand years, guided the Trojan hero Aeneas to Avernus, as the realm below was called, through a volcanic fissure in the area of Mt. Vesuvius. There Aeneas met heroes of the past and saw those of the future, as yet unborn. It is said that some centuries later that same Sibyl offered nine books of prophecy to King Tarquin at a price that he thought was far too high. So she burned three and offered the remaining six at the same price. When Tarquin again refused, she burned three more and still asked the original price for the last three. Then the king, realizing his mistake, bought the three books, which thereafter were kept in the Temple of Jupiter in Rome and consulted as oracles in times of national emergency. Whenever the Sibylline Books failed to yield an answer, the blame was placed on King Tarquin, for the assumption was that one of the lost books could have provided it. But the Sibyl still ranked high in Roman estimation, even though the books that she allegedly burned could very well have been blanks.

This legend shows how witchcraft was acknowledged and esteemed in ancient Rome. It has been linked with the worship of Diana, the goddess of the moon, but it really belongs to Hecate, who was Diana's antithesis. Whereas Diana danced in the moonlight, Hecate skulked in the dark of the moon. What happened there in the darkness was dastardly, indeed. The Roman poet Horace gives a graphic description of two haggard crones stalking the Esquiline cemetery, gathering ingredients for a witch's brew. That done, they wailed a wild chant to Hecate, followed by the slaughter of a black lamb, whose blood was poured into a pit to invoke departed spirits. As snakes and hell-hounds appeared, one of the witches threw a wax image representing a victim into a blazing fire. As it melted to the accompaniment of hideous howls from fleeting ghosts, so did the life of the intended victim wane.

The witch's brew itself served various purposes, and the more unsavory its contents, the better the results. One such concoction, used for rejuvenation, was attributed to a legendary witch named Medea. It included the dried skin of a water snake, hoar frost gathered by moonlight, the head and wings of an owl, the entrails of a wolf, chunks of tortoise shell, the head and beak of an ancient crow, the liver from a living stag, and other items too unpalatable to mention. Medea stirred the mixture with a dried branch of an olive tree, which promptly bloomed, proving that the potion could restore youth to a human being as well, which it did when properly administered.

Tales of this kind have been cited as evidence that witchcraft cannot be all bad; but more to the point, it cannot be all good, either. From the time of Medea, ancient witches had a way of tricking people into quaffing what they thought was something pleasant, like a love potion, when in fact they had gulped a deadly poison, the slower acting the better, as it gave the witch more time to taunt the dying victim.

A noted authority on Etruscan lore, Charles G. Leland, aptly summed up the subject of witchcraft with the comment, "The farther back we go, the darker and more vindictive it becomes." It is quite easy to trace many seemingly innocent practices of today back to roots of a truly insidious sort. Always, too, there is the prospect of some almost forgotten ancient rite erupting into some modern madness, just as Medea's dried tree branch burst into fruitful bloom.

One striking phase of witchcraft that has been recurrent since antiquity is that of turning human beings into animals or vice versa. The legendary pioneer in that practice was a princess named Circe. Banished to a lonely island for murdering her husband, she sought revenge by transforming visiting navigators into lions, tigers, wolves, and eventually pigs. Some have questioned whether these transformations were actual, or whether they took place only in the minds of the victims or persons who saw them; either way, this could have indicated the use of hypnotic suggestion or the effect of drugs, both of which figured in Roman witchcraft of a later era.

Belief in witchcraft had reached large proportions by the year A.D. 160, when a Roman author named Lucius Apuleius wrapped it all up in a story called *The Golden Ass*, which was related as a series of personal adventures and readily accepted as fact by the superstitious readers of that period. In the course of his adventures, Apuleius traveled into a region of Greece where witchcraft was notoriously rampant. Stopping at the home of a wealthy man named Milo, he became enamored of Fotis, a serving maid, who confidentially informed him that Milo's wife, Pamphile, was a witch and frequently turned herself into a bird and took off on nocturnal flights to meet with others of her ilk. All agog, Lucius persuaded Fotis to provide him with a hiding place from which he could watch her mistress undergo such a transformation.

Fotis agreed and Lucius watched Pamphile disrobe and cover her body with a special ointment that she took from a jar. As she shook herself, she began to sprout feathers; her nose became a beak, her toes turned into claws, and her arms took on the shape of wings. As she uttered a loud screech, Lucius saw to his amazement that she had changed completely into a huge owl. Moments later, she had flown out the window.

Here the narrator interpolated the touch that made his story seem valid. He felt that either his senses had completely left him, or that he himself was the one who was bewitched — a line of reasoning that was to persist through later centuries, when persons like Pamphile were accused of witchcraft. Whether such transformations were real, or whether they took place only in the minds of the onlookers, the accused would be blamed and forced to take the consequences.

When Lucius "came back to himself," as he aptly put it, he decided to make the only sure test. He persuaded Fotis to bring him the ointment so that he, too, could become an owl and go flying off to learn what was happening in the world of witches. Naturally, he wanted to be sure that he could be transformed back into himself when he returned, and Fotis assured him that such a process would be simple — she would give him a drink of water flavored with laurel leaves, which she always had ready for her mistress when she returned. That was the sure antidote for the charm.

So Lucius shed his clothes and anointed himself lavishly, but when he flapped his arms, hoping to fly, he found that his hands, instead of sprouting feathers from their fingertips, were hardening into a solid mass. His feet and toes were doing the same, his face and jaws were becoming wide and monstrous and his ears long and hairy. When he tried to utter an impressive screech, he brayed instead. Fotis had brought the wrong jar. Lucius had become a donkey.

Though tempted to kick Fotis into oblivion, Lucius restrained himself, since she was his only hope. He listened patiently while she told him that if he ate some rose petals, he would become himself again. Unfortunately, Fotis had neglected to pluck any roses during the day, but she promised to bring some in the morning. So Lucius went to the stable and picked himself a stall for the night, thinking his problems would soon be over.

Instead, they had only begun. During the night, a band of robbers broke into the house, found Milo's treasure chest, and looted it. Their plunder was far more than they could carry, so they loaded the bulk of it on Lucius and another donkey that they found in the stable. Then they headed for the hills. Lucius, the donkey who could do everything but talk, was embarked on a series of frustrating adventures that ended only when he resorted to silent prayer and was fed some roses by a kindly priest of Isis.

The Golden Ass, while replete with satire and ribaldry, still stands as a monumental landmark in the history of witchcraft, because Lucius Apuleius personally learned it the hard way. Born in Africa, he studied law in Rome and religion in Greece, and returned to Libya, where he married a rich widow. Soon her relatives were accusing Apuleius of having used witchcraft to win her love, and of poisoning her son in order to take over her estate.

Apuleius was charged with applying that ancient whammy, the Evil Eye, to several Libyan youths, and brought to trial. But his accusers were able to produce only one victim. Apuleius, acting in his own defence, calmly presented evidence to prove that the boy had been addicted to fits before he had met him. He was also accused of possessing a special image of the sort used in witchcraft, but when he offered it as an exhibit, close examination showed it to be a miniature statue of the god Mercury, whom Apuleius had every right to worship.

In short, the case was virtually laughed out of court, but nobody laughed off witchcraft itself, especially Apuleius. His acquittal was the one-in-a-thousand that pointed to the guilt of the nine hundred and ninety-nine who were not smart enough to keep a jump ahead of their accusers.

One reason why the witches of antiquity frequented cemeteries was because there they could obtain parts of newly buried bodies to use in mixing brews and ointments. It was much better, of course, to get at the bodies before they were buried, but that could be very difficult if close watch was kept over a corpse until the time of its interment. Still, the wily witches found ways to accomplish their gruesome aim.

According to an authoritative account by Apuleius, a young man was once hired to watch over a body during the night. Warned that any witches seeking to dismember it might come and go in the form of animals, birds, or even insects, he was particularly on the lookout for dogs or mice, as they were creatures that would cause the least suspicion, but all he spotted was a small weasel, which he chased away whenever it appeared. Between times, he noted that the corpse was undisturbed, so when people arrived in the morning, he proudly boasted that his vigil had succeeded. But close scrutiny in the daylight showed that the nose, lips and ears had been skillfully severed from the dead face and replaced with replicas made from wax. One or more witches, playing the part of a weasel, had done the ghoulish job piecemeal, covering each step before taking the next.

Such hideous practices are associated with a special breed of ancient witches known as Lamias. Lamia, a legendary queen of Libya, had had her children stolen by the goddess Juno. Thereupon Lamia began to kill other children and so gained the power of perpetual rejuvenation by feasting on human blood. A "Lamia" thus came to mean any witch or demon with similar proclivities, and therefore is generally recognized as the forerunner of the modern vampire.

Whether demon or human, a Lamia used witchcraft to assume a seductive beauty that would lure susceptible youths into her power. Apollonius of Tyana, a philosophical mystic who slightly antedated Lucius Apuleius, was credited with breaking up the wedding of a young man named Menippus and a beautiful woman from Corinth by denouncing the bride-to-be as the Lamia she really was.

That was easy then, and still is, provided you can apply a whammy of your own. Apollonius had the formula. All he had to do was prove that beauty was only skin deep by snatching away the Lamia's mask and revealing either the leering visage of a hellish demon or the haggard countenance of a superannuated witch. Either way, Apollonius could not lose. But still, the Lamia beat him to the punch. She gave a shriek and disappeared intact, along with the sumptuous surroundings of the wedding party that she had provided, including a host of servants as nebulous as herself.

If all these tales read like a flashback to an age of myth and fable, it is. But every item so far mentioned had a deep significance for the future. Some of these ancient practices have continued through until today and may carry over to tomorrow, perhaps even more strongly than before.

2
The Druids and Their Legends

As the Roman Empire spread, so did Roman ideas and traditions, among them witchcraft. It did not just have to go with the Romans; sometimes it was there ahead of them, waiting, willing, and wanting them to catch up with it which, naturally, they did. Often the Romans identified the local gods in terms of their own, for the fact that the Romans were the victors proved that the gods were on their side, and that in itself was sufficient reason for the vanquished nations to accept the Roman rule. In short, Roman domination was furthered by making due allowance for the superstitions of the conquered peoples; and that included witchcraft.

One notable exception was Britain, where the real rulers consisted of a cult of robed and bearded mystics called Druids, who practiced potent witchcraft of their own. They performed their rites out of doors, either amid great circles of massive stone monuments, such as those at Avesbury and Stonehenge, or in the shelter of sacred groves of oak trees. The Druids were supposedly the offshoots of a much earlier race of sun worshippers, the real builders of the monuments; but it was definitely known that the Druids themselves practiced a fire ritual in which human beings were sacrificed. Only desperate criminals were supposed to be thrown into the flames, but there was no telling what the Druids might do if they ran out of such timber. Then, any hapless person might be sacrificed.

That, at least, was the argument the Romans used against the Druids. What really worried the Romans were the claims the Druids made; claims which their followers implicitly accepted. Supposedly, the Druids could turn people into stones, like the circles of monoliths where they held their rites. They could raise fogs and create clouds from which they could bring down showers of fire and even blood. They could cause darkness and floods, provide antidotes for poisoned darts, and, best of all, produce tempests strong enough to scatter any enemy fleet that dared approach their shores.

When Julius Caesar invaded Britain in 55 B.C., he met with resistance from the moment he landed, largely because the Britons relied on the Druids to back them. Once established, Caesar sent for cavalry to reinforce his army but, true to form, the Druids raised a tempest that scattered the Roman fleet as it neared the shore, wrecking the ships so badly that the Romans barely managed to piece enough together to withdraw their forces to the mainland.

Caesar came back in 54 B.C., so fully arrayed that the Britons retired before his army's advance. But when they finally gave battle, another tempest — of Druid origin, no doubt! — drove the Romans back to the coast and forced them to begin all over. Caesar termed this expedition a "conquest," but after the tribes submitted one by one, he left Britain and never returned; nor did the Romans attack the island again for nearly a hundred years.

Then, in the wake of a new invasion, the Emperor Claudius arrived with a force so formidable that resistance was impossible. He occupied the native capital of Camulodunum (now the city of

Colchester), and Roman legions fanned out from the site of modern London, establishing encampments, encouraging settlers, and driving the Druids into the remote hinterlands. Claudius, on his return to Rome, was honored as a god under the name of Brittanicus in recognition of this achievement.

To give the Britons some form of worship, a temple to Claudius was erected in Camulodunum, with a statue of Victory in its midst. That was a double insult. Brought up to worship nature in the great outdoors, the Britons could not comprehend the confinement of a god within a temple; and the mere sight of Victory in frozen, statuesque form, made them realize that they, the vanquished, were still very much alive. They only wished the Druids would do something about it.

So the Druids did.

One sunny day in Camulodunum, the statue of Victory toppled from its pedestal, landed flat on its face and cracked apart. The Britons, knowing nothing of leverage, gunpowder, TNT, or atomic energy, did not have to *guess* why it happened, because they *knew* why it did. The Druids did it — and that was that.

So revolt broke out all over Britain. Everything that the Romans had established was torn down, including the Temple of Claudius, alias *Deus Brittanicus*. However, after the Romans pulled themselves out of the ruins of everything, including Londinium, as they then called London, they went out to find the Druids.

They found them on the Isle of Mona, off the northwest coast of Wales. The island, now called Anglesey, was separated from the mainland by a narrow channel easily crossed by flat-bottomed boats. As the first wave of Romans landed, they were met by a motley army, consisting of the Druids themselves, surrounded by their hard-core followers, including black-clad women with disheveled hair, who rushed about screaming like the Furies and brandishing lighted torches in the faces of the foe.

The robed Druids topped it by raising their hands and eyes to heaven and delivering a loud, weird chant to bring down fire from the sky. Thus encouraged, their armed followers charged the stupefied Romans and would have driven them back into the water but for the fact that new boatloads of arrivals goaded the front ranks forward. The Romans went into action and, when the heavens failed to deliver the anticipated fire, the result was a wholesale slaughter of the Druids and their fanatical followers.

The Romans established an encampment on the island and chopped down the sacred grove where the Druids had held their rites. Though their power as a cult was broken, the scattered remnants of the Druids continued to practice witchcraft and hold secret ceremonies in caverns and forests throughout the remote provinces that marked the fringe of Roman domination, which ended about the year 400. But by then Christianity had gained a hold in Britain, so there was no strong reversion to Druidism.

Instead, many Druid traditions were absorbed into British folklore, along with Roman superstitions, thereby accounting for tales of elves, gnomes, goblins and various forms of fairy folk. These traditions were mixed with the primitive beliefs of the Angles and the Saxons who invaded Britain after the departure of the Romans, driving many of the native Britons into exile. In the course of a few centuries, these newcomers blended with the populace and adopted Christian ways, but many of the old customs still prevailed.

The centuries from the year 500 to 1000 have been aptly termed the "Dark Ages" of European history, due to the disintegration of the Roman Empire and the culture that it represented. So many valuable artifacts and records, which could have shed light on the era, were destroyed by barbarian hordes, that whatever records did remain were a mingling of fact and fancy. English history provides an outstanding example of this blending in the Arthurian Legend, which is of special interest here because it is replete with tales of witchcraft that bridge the gap between ancient and modern beliefs and superstitions.

The real King Arthur was probably a British commander in the service of the Romans, who rallied the native chieftains about him when the legions were withdrawn, thus becoming the nominal king of a temporarily united Britain. The coalition apparently held off the early Teutonic invaders during Arthur's reign, but later, the Britons were driven to the wilds of Wales and Cornwall, from where many eventually sailed for the French coastal region of Armorica, across the English Channel, and founded a colony from which the name Brittany is derived.

Thus, as bards sang the praises of King Arthur through the ensuing centuries, they wove in tales of other heroes until a mighty monarch emerged as head of a heroic band of knights whose exploits were drawn from Roman, Briton, Welsh, Breton, Anglo-Saxon and even Scandinavian lore. By the year 1100, English historians were accepting many of these composite claims as facts and describing the court of King Arthur in terms of the rising chivalry of their own period. But the tales of witchcraft came from those earlier days and their fanciful notions still persisted.

The Arthurian Legend centered about a mythical wizard named Merlin, who packed as much mystic power as a whole den of Druids. He was credited with having transported the huge stone monoliths at Stonehenge from some remote spot across the sea. It was Merlin who provided a marble block containing a mysteriously imbedded sword which Arthur drew from the stone to prove his right to the throne.

King Arthur and his knights frequently encountered witchcraft, good and bad, in the course of their adventures. Once, King Arthur met a warlock disguised as a knight, who suggested a duel in which each, in turn, would have a chance to chop off his opponent's head. He gave King Arthur first turn, and with a single stroke, the king sent the warlock's head rolling on the floor; but the warlock's body sprang after it and his hands placed it back on his neck as good as ever.

The pretended knight gave King Arthur a year to put his affairs in order, before taking his turn to be beheaded. To worry Arthur further, the warlock posed a riddle: What is it that a woman desires most in the world? If the king came back with the right answer, he would call off the duel. All during the year, King Arthur pondered the riddle with the knights of his Round Table, but none of their guesses sounded satisfactory. So at the end of the year he set out for his appointment with doom, with little hope of returning.

On the way, the king met a weird old witch who not only recognized him, but knew of his problem and the answer to the riddle. That which a woman most desires, the old crone cackled, is to have her will. Aiding Arthur even more, she also revealed the secret of the warlock's immunity to sword strokes. Instead of carrying his life in his body, the imitation knight kept it in a small crystal ball inside a large locket that hung from a chain around his neck. At the warlock's castle, King Arthur answered the riddle, snatched the locket from the warlock's neck and broke the crystal it contained, whereupon the conniving warlock dropped dead.

The amulet of the Arthurian legend may have its roots in Druid witchcraft, for they wore large beads of striped colored glass, called "adder eggs" or "snake stones," which they claimed were generated by serpents and could only be gathered on a certain day of the moon. These, when worn, were regarded as charms against various ailments, sometimes even death. As for the life of a person residing in such an object rather than his own body, that notion of an "external soul" could have been brought to England by the Romans, for it is found in ancient Italian witch lore. Or it might have come from Norway via the Hebrides Islands, for it belongs to Norse legend, too; while other fantastic versions have been told throughout the Orient.

As a reward for giving King Arthur the warlock's secret, the old witch demanded the right to marry a knight of the Round Table. When she chose Sir Gawain, King Arthur's nephew, he not only accepted his fate, but treated the old crone with all the courtesy due a bride. The respect Gawain accorded the crone broke a spell that had bewitched her and she turned back into the beautiful woman she was originally. This, too, was typical of the witchcraft of the period.

Beautifully bewitching women abound in Arthurian lore, and sometimes even the power of a sorcerer's magic meets its match at a fair woman's hand, as Merlin himself found to be true. Merlin's first — and most regrettable — mistake was to choose a damsel named Vivien as an apprentice. Once having learned his secrets, Vivien wasted no time in binding Merlin with one of his own spells. So doing, she went on her merry way and established herself in an enchanted castle with a retinue of servants — and there began her woeful deeds. ... Vivien attended a tournament which was won by a knight named Sir Sagron; but instead of being swayed by Vivien's wiles, he bestowed the victor's chaplet upon a local beauty, the Lady Lesolie. Viven, greatly piqued, promptly put an enchantment on a fountain near Lady Lesolie's castle, so that if anyone poured water on a slab beside it, a violent storm would arise and deluge the area.

When a knight in quest of adventure stopped at Vivien's castle, she slyly directed him to the enchanted fountain where he unwittingly raised a storm by pouring water on the slab. Promptly Sir Sagron arrived and challenged him to combat, in behalf of the Lady Lesolie, whose domain had been damaged.

A knight of the Round Table, Sir Uwaine, undertook the adventure at Vivien's instigation; and in the conflict that followed, Sir Sagron finally met more than his match. When Sir Uwaine nearly unhorsed him with a tremendous sword stroke, Sir Sagron, realizing he had suffered a mortal blow, fled for the safety of Lady Lesolie's castle. Sir Uwaine pursued him through the entrance, where the warder let the portcullis fall, killing Uwaine's horse and trapping him within a grilled gate.

That night, while Sir Sagron lay dying, a damsel named Elose approached the gate and slipped Uwaine a ruby ring, telling him to wear it with the stone turned inward. Uwaine did and became invisible, so that in the morning, when men-at-arms opened the gate to look for him, he walked out safely and unseen. Uwaine later returned the magic ring to Elose and she introduced him to the Lady Lesolie, to whom he offered his services as Defender of the Fountain, as a replacement for the dead Sir Sagron.

A romance developed between Uwaine and Lesolie, but as their wedding day approached, he felt it his duty to make a brief trip to Camelot and report to King Arthur. On the way, he made the mistake of stopping at Vivien's castle; and the sorceress, as a pledge of her friendship and good faith — elements entirely lacking in her nature — gave him a ring with a yellow stone, probably a chrysolite, which immediately caused him to forget all that had happened since his previous visit. So Uwaine might never have returned to claim his bride, but for the fact that he stopped overnight at a hut frequented by a band of thieves, who attacked him while he slept and robbed him of all his valuables, including the ring of forgetfulness. Immediately he recalled the Lady Lesolie and returned to her castle and married her, despite Vivien's treachery.

Those were but two forms of belief in the power of magic rings, out of dozens dating from ancient times, with various gems figuring in other forms of witchcraft, such as giving immunity to poison, inspiring happy dreams, increasing wisdom and improving eyesight. In contrast, some could bring misfortune, like Vivien's gift to Uwaine, but that was something the donor never mentioned.

If the skeptics of the Arthurian Era needed anything to convince them that witchcraft existed, nature itself provided the affirmative answer. Just as the Roman god Jupiter hurled down his shafts of lightning, so did Thor, the Teutonic thunder god, but usually with a louder rumble. Eclipses of the sun or moon, appearances of the aurora borealis, otherwise known as the northern lights, and other such natural phenomena were also attributed to supernatural forces.

One of the most notable cases in point involved King Arthur's sister, Morgana Le Fay, who was almost as well-versed in witchcraft as Merlin. She and her followers were supposed to dwell on a floating island called Avalon, which drifted far out to sea, but occasionally came so close to shore that it could be seen from the mainland. Observers gazed in awe at the castellated walls of the mystic city, with turrets and towers surrounded by green groves and sloping lawns. Often, viewers claimed that they heard elfin voices raised in song, coming across the placid sea from Avalon; but that touch was sheer imagination.

What they thought was a fairy isle was actually a mirage, the inverted image of some headland, such as Land's End or another

British promontory, whose cliffs produced the illusion of towering walls rising above grassy, tree-studded slopes. Word of that enchanted land spread far during the years and Morgana must have decided to steer Avalon southward during the winter season, for the floating island made occasional appearances in the Straits of Messina, between Italy and Sicily, usually being viewed from the Italian town of Reggio, where it was known by the name of Fata Morgana.

According to legend, when King Arthur was mortally wounded in battle, Morgana Le Fay carried him by boat to Avalon, where he is supposedly still living, due to the potency of her witchcraft, waiting for the day when Britain will need his services again. Meanwhile, the Isle of Avalon has extended its cruising range, for only about half a century ago, strollers on the boardwalk at Atlantic City saw the Fata Morgana floating offshore in all its castellated glory.

Apparently, Morgana had either improved her witchcraft or had put propellers on Avalon in order to make a transatlantic voyage. But such notions faded away like the isle itself, when experts on mirages identified it as the reflected image of Rehobeth Beach, Delaware, a resort located south of the New Jersey coast.

An equally fantastic phenomenon, dating from the days of the Druids, or earlier, concerns the gigantic guardians of the Brocken, the highest peak of the Harz Mountains in Saxony. There, witches galore were supposed to assemble on May Day and Midsummer Eve to perform ancient rites akin to those attributed to the Druids at Stonehenge. Other summits served as similar gathering places, but the Brocken was the most fearful of all. Among the grotesque formations of granite found there are the "Witch's Chair" and the "Devil's Pulpit," which undoubtedly had earlier names of equally grim significance.

In contrast to the Isle of Avalon, which no ordinary mortal could even approach, the Brocken was easily accessible. But no one dared to climb it, except in broadest daylight, for the King of the Brocken took charge at night and sometimes his huge, spectral figure could be seen looming from the mists that gathered in the early dawn, occasionally flanked by equally formidable companions. Sight of such towering guardians invariably scared away the boldest climbers; and all during the period of witchcraft persecutions in Germany, which began about 1500 and persisted for nearly three centuries, the legend of the Brocken grew in proportion to the size of its weird custodians.

It was not until comparatively modern times that this strange phenomenon was both confirmed and explained almost simultaneously. Mountain climbers, who no longer believed in witchcraft, began ascending the Brocken to view the sunrise; and an inn was established there to accommodate them overnight. One man who happened to get up early caught the reflection of the sunrise from low hanging clouds and mist; there, to his amazement, he saw the huge specter, bigger even than the fanciful reports. A wind was stirring and, as the man recoiled, it blew away his hat. He made an instinctive grab and the mammoth figure did the same.

The viewer knew then that he was looking at a projected image of himself, magnified against the mist where it was cast. He hurriedly summoned the innkeeper and when they reached the spot where he had seen the specter, two were there to greet them and mimic all their actions. That explained why superstitious witnesses of an earlier period had seen two or more such phantom shapes. The more viewers, the more reflections, and therefore the more giants.

Of such stuff are legends made, particularly when witchcraft is supposedly involved. But many centuries were to pass before the age of science dawned to counteract such beliefs. What happened during those years between, our next chapters will reveal.

3
Witchcraft Comes of Age

When Europe emerged from the Dark Ages in the year A.D. 1000, the art of witchcraft took on as many aspects as there were customs of the countries to which it spread. Among other things, witchcraft became either the toy or the tool of the ruling classes, and for a time, it was tolerated; that is, until it raised problems that demanded drastic action.

In the centuries encompassing the Roman Empire, stern edicts against witchcraft were essential soon after the establishment of Christianity as the state religion, for witchcraft represented a return to the worship of Diana, whose very existence, along with the rest of the Greek and Roman pantheon, was no longer recognized. But in England, France, and Germany, it marked a merging of Roman and local traditions that promised to cancel each other out when Christianity increased its hold.

An interesting case of how Roman methods of witchcraft were adapted by the English is found in the tale of Sir Marrok, which though legendary, is an accurate recital of the superstitious beliefs and practices in England, from the Arthurian era on. Sir Marrok, off for the Saxon wars, left the Lady Irma (whom he married after his first wife's death) in charge of his castle and his young son. When reports arrived of Marrok's death in battle, Irma dismissed his trusted servants and sent the boy away to parts unknown, intending to take over the castle for her own.

Unexpectedly, Sir Marrok returned, alive. Lady Irma received him cordially, explained that his son was asleep and offered him a goblet of spiced wine. As he drank, grayish hair spread on his face, which in turn became a muzzle, and his hands and feet were transformed into paws. He landed bewildered on all fours and saw himself reflected in a mirror as a lean gray wolf. Before he could turn on the woman who had bewitched him, her shrill call brought a squad of armed retainers and the wolf was lucky to outrun them from the castle and escape into the surrounding forest.

During the ensuing years, the great gray wolf not only eluded all hunters; he outfought the biggest wolves he encountered and drove their packs from the forest. He also sprang surprise attacks on outlaws, killing enough to discourage others from remaining in that vicinity. He even set fire to the huts of warlocks and witches who served Lady Irma. But he was wise enough never to venture near the castle.

Then late one afternoon, the bewitched Marrok saw a young knight riding toward the castle and from his accoutrements, the observant wolf decided that it was his own son, come back to claim his patrimony. Knowing the fate that awaited the youth, Marrok desperately pawed his way to a secret exit from the castle that he had avoided during all those years. He worked his way up to an underground chamber and there he found his own sword, cloak and armor on permanent exhibit, across from a shelf where a wax image of an owl gazed unblinkingly from above three lighted candles, colored respectively red, green and blue. But above, on a higher shelf, stood the hardened figurine of a lone gray wolf. With one swing of his forepaw, Sir Marrok knocked the clay image from its perch, and as it cracked on the stone floor, he became — this time not to his surprise — his own familiar self, Sir Marrok.

Grabbing his cloak and sword, Sir Marrok rushed up to the great hall, where he found Lady Irma proffering a chalice to the young knight, saying, "Pledge me in this wine, Sir Knight, and I shall tell thee where to find thy father." No pledge was needed. Papa was already there, swinging his sword toward the chalice, hoping to break it. But Irma, fast as ever, was ahead of him. She snatched it away, gulped its contents and flew hooting out through a high window that she had fortunately left open as a quick exit for Marrok's son.

This furnishes a good clue to what was going on in England at that time. Spiced wine that turned knights into wolves or witches into owls were slightly on the fantastic side; but there were more prosaic concoctions as well, such as love philtres and death potions, with a whole range of mixtures that served in-between purposes and worked slowly or swiftly, as preferred, but always surely.

In later centuries, these brews were to gain recognition on their own merits, but during the Middle Ages they were generally regarded as adjuncts to witchcraft, with their potency depending on gruesome ingredients stirred at the right time of the moon. When administered, they were usually fortified by a glare of the Evil Eye or the muttering of some mumbo jumbo that served as an incantation.

While the secrets of witchcraft could be taught to willing pupils, contact with more virulent sources was essential to make the initiate function to his fullest; and sometimes warlocks and witches cropped up so unexpectedly that they appeared to be self-made. With Diana and her sinister opposite, Hecate, branded as myths along with the Norse and Teutonic deities, theologians were confronted with a real dilemma. To class witchcraft itself as sheer imagination would be to deny the potency that it obviously possessed. To allow its practice would be a direct reversion toward the outlawed pagan worship with which it was so solidly linked.

So they blamed it on the Devil, as head of a horde of demons and lesser imps, whose activities expanded in proportion to the reported facts that could be attributed to them. Any assemblage of witches could thus be condemned as a form of devil-worship, but it was quite as easy for anyone to form an individual pact with the Devil or one of his subordinates. Among the latter was a specific type of male demon known as an *incubus*, which supposedly haunted women in their sleep; and to whose nocturnal forays the birth of witches and warlocks was attributed. The female equivalent of the *incubus* was called a *succuba* and caused similar problems where men were concerned.

Vivid nightmares were often blamed on these demons, although they may have served as alibis where actual lechery was involved. Their prevalence was partly explained by the claim that a group of incubi and succubae had long ago taken over an island in the Mediterranean as their very own and that the present inhabitants were therefore a race of full-fledged demons, capable of taking off on flights throughout the world and doing their usual mischief wherever they happened to land.

Confirmation of such theories was built into the Merlin legend. It is told that the Devil approached a pious young woman during an unguarded moment and thus Merlin was engendered. The purpose of this liaison was to provide the world with a human fiend possessed of such hellish powers that he could stop the rising tide of Christianity; but an alert priest baptized the infant Merlin so promptly after birth that his Satanic sire was thwarted. Merlin still possessed his diabolical talents, but instead of using them for evil, he became the champion do-gooder of his era.

Shortly after the year 1000, a similar, but far more plausible story was built around a real-life personage, Robert, Duke of Normandy, popularly known as "Robert the Devil." His mother, wanting another child and finding that prayers were to no avail, implored the Devil to grant her wish. Robert was born soon afterward and though generally conceded to be the true son of the current duke, he acted as though he were the Devil's own. He was reputedly versed in witchcraft and even in his youth, he became both the hero and the villain of fantastic adventures that studded his singularly sinful and ferocious career. His brother, Richard, inherited the dukedom in 1026 and when he died mysteriously two years later, Robert took over in his stead.

Whether Richard died from poison or witchcraft (which often were one and the same), Robert was generally suspected of the crime, although it was never proven. However, several years later, he set out on a pilgrimage to the Holy Land, which was regarded as a form of penance. As his successor, he named his young son William, whose mother was a tanner's daughter who had succumbed to Robert's blandishments during one of his devilish misadventures. Robert died while in Syria and William became Duke of Normandy, later to claim the throne of England and gain it as William the Conqueror.

William, too, was frequently suspected of using witchcraft to achieve his aims. Duke Alain of Brittany, who acted as regent during William's minority, died very suddenly; and years later, when William was about to embark for the conquest of England, Alain's son, Conan, turned against him, claiming that Alain should have been the rightful ruler of Normandy, but that William had poisoned him. Rather than leave Normandy open to attack by Duke Conan, William sent conciliatory messages back and forth by a mutual friend and trouble was averted.

Shortly thereafter, an infection appeared on Conan's hands and when he unthinkingly stroked his face, it spread there, too, so rapidly that he soon died from the effects of a mysterious and virulent poison. His followers were of the opinion that while Conan was preparing a reply to William's last message, the messenger sprinkled a special powder in the duke's gloves and on his horse's reins. But the charge remained unproven.

Other rumors, however, were equally to William's discredit. The province of Maine was ruled by Count Herbert, whose brother Walter, the next in line, died quite suddenly. Soon afterward, Count Herbert also died under mysterious circumstances, and with Walter already gone, the province went to William.

So it was little wonder that Duke William was generally regarded as a worthy son of "Robert the Devil" and the illegitimacy of his birth added to the sinister touch. All through his life, luck and omens favored him and he made the most of them. In 1066, he timed his invasion of England to the appearance of a great comet and it proved to be his lucky star. When he landed on the English coast, he tripped as he came ashore and a moan came from the superstitious Normans, who took it to be a bad sign. But the moans changed to cheers when William came to his feet, clutching a fistful of sand and proclaiming it a token that all the remaining land of England would be his, which it rapidly became.

Yet William, like his father, affected a pious attitude that would have disclaimed witchcraft entirely, if he hadn't used it when the time was ripe. A die-hard Saxon named Hereward, popularly termed "Hereward the Wake," defied the Normans until they drove him to the Isle of Ely, in the heart of the marshy fenlands. When the Normans tried to build causeways to get at Hereward, his men sprang up apparently from nowhere, with sudden attacks that smacked of witchcraft.

To counteract that, William, ever resourceful, and perhaps equally sure of his diabolic ancestry, ordered a tower to be built in the heart of the disputed fenlands. There, he installed a resident witch whose job was to overwhelm the fenlanders with spells more powerful than any they could produce. Good thinking on William's part, as he probably figured that the Saxons hadn't any worthwhile spells to begin with.

Except they didn't need spells. They simply crawled through the rushes, and set fire to them, directly under the wooden tower, sending it up in flames and taking the witch along with it. By the time the Normans had recovered from the shock, the incendiaries were off through the brakes to rejoin Hereward on his final flight from the fens. That was one witch burning that was really justified.

The pattern of witchcraft in high places was strongly evidenced during the next few centuries, but its constant tendency was to spread to lower circles of society. As robber barons and feudal lords rose to the rank of kings, they passed laws against its practice, often for their own protection, since they had become so powerful that witchcraft was one of the few remaining ways their rivals could undermine them.

When such attempts were made, the instigators, in their turn, generally delegated the work to subordinates or secret accomplices, so as to be clear of blame if things backfired. Also, if they believed in witchcraft, they preferred to leave it to hands more skillful than their own; while if they doubted it and were merely plotting an insurrection or assassination, a pretence of witchcraft was a good way to play on the gullibility of their followers and rouse them to fanatical action.

Most attractive of all, from the standpoint of the lawmakers themselves, was the chance this gave them to beat prospective plotters to the punch by the simple expedient of accusing them of doing the very thing they would have liked to do. Persons paid to spread rumors of a plot would name higher ups from whom confessions, wrung by torture, named those still higher, until it reached the level of someone whose property it would be worth confiscating.

The best way to appreciate the viciousness of this circle is through a brief survey of some of the more spectacular witchcraft cases as reported in the early years of the fourteenth century:

In the year 1323, some shepherd dogs attracted attention at a cross-roads on the outskirts of Paris, where they kept whining and digging at a patch of ground despite all efforts to call them off. Their owners dug there and pried up some stones under which they found a strongly constructed box containing a large black cat with a supply of food and some articles used in religious rites. Two tubes ran from the box to the ground above, furnishing the cat with air; and the scent from those had caused the dogs to dig.

The police were notified and questioned all the carpenters in the surrounding villages until they found one who remembered making the box for a man named Jean Prevost. Prevost was arrested and after being given the customary torture, he admitted that he and an accomplice named De Persant had been employed by the Abbot of Sarcelles to find out who had stolen some money from him and that they were using witchcraft for that purpose.

Their procedure called for leaving the cat in the box for three days, then killing it and cutting its skin into long, thin strips so as to form a charmed circle. From within the circle, they were to invoke a demon called Berich; and once he appeared, he would reveal the desired details.

The fact that they had been forestalled before going through with the malevolent ceremony apparently delayed the trial, for Prevost died before it was completed; but De Persant was convicted soon afterward and was burned alive, along with the body of his dead partner in witchcraft. The abbot, though perhaps more a dupe than a guilty party, was sentenced to prison along with some other persons who admitted knowing of the transaction.

In the year 1323, when England was suffering under the misrule of King Edward II and his chief advisor, Hugh Despenser, and the latter's son, also named Hugh, a group of men in Coventry turned to witchcraft as a means to end the nation's woes. Headed by a man named Richard Latoner, they chose Hallowe'en as an appropriate night to visit John of Nottingham, a veteran warlock, and make a proposal which he readily accepted.

John was supplied with wax, canvas and other materials, along with enough food for several months, so that he and an accomplice named Robert Mareschal could set up shop in an old deserted manor house outside Coventry. The place, which was reputedly haunted, was ideal for their clandestine operations, which involved the fashioning of lifelike images of their prospective victims. These were seven in all: King Edward, the two Despensers, the Prior of Coventry and two lesser prelates, with an extra figurine representing a court favorite named Richard de Sowe, who was chosen for experimental purposes, since he was generally detested.

The warlock and his apprentice must have gathered many weird ingredients from graveyards and elsewhere during baleful periods of the moon, for their work was not completed until the following spring. The figures, too, were exact to the last detail, even including a miniature crown on the head of the image representing the king. Late one spring night, after all was complete, John of Nottingham showed Robert Mareschal a curiously fashioned pin made of pure lead and thrust it into the head of the experimental puppet.

In the morning, John told Robert to stop by the house where Richard de Sowe lived and find out how the witchcraft was doing. It was doing very well, but Richard wasn't. He had awakened screaming in the night and was now practically out of his mind, unable to recognize anyone. His delirium continued intermittently during the next three weeks, until John of Nottingham decided to ease Richard's torment.

Again with Robert Mareschal as witness, the warlock drew the curious pin from the puppet's head; then, as an afterthought, he thrust it into the figure's heart. Next day, when Robert stopped at the de Sowe house, he learned that Richard's delirium had ended, but that he was confined to bed, suffering from severe chest pains. Three days later, Richard de Sowe died, apparently from a heart attack.

All was then ready to begin work on the figures of the king and his ministers, much to the joy of Richard Latoner and his two dozen associates. But they, along with John of Nottingham, had overlooked the weak link in their chain — Robert Mareschal; either his frequent calls at the de Sowe house had roused suspicion by the authorities, or he had been so shaken by the result of John of Nottingham's witchcraft that he went to the constabulary himself and revealed the whole conspiracy.

Mass arrests followed. John of Nottingham and Robert Mareschal were charged with murder by witchcraft; but Richard Latoner and his associates denied any complicity, so the trial was delayed until some time in 1325. By then, John of Nottingham had conveniently died in jail and although Robert Mareschal was sentenced to a prison term, his unsupported testimony was not enough to convict Richard Latoner or any of his group.

There was still the matter of conspiring against the life of King Edward II and his principal ministers, the Despensers, who all were anxious to press charges against the Coventry plotters. But more delays followed and, by the end of 1326, a revolt of the English barons resulted in the capture and execution of both Despensers, followed by the deposition and murder of Edward II in Berkeley Castle the next year. So, seemingly, crime triumphed over witchcraft, or vice versa, though the two could have been hand in glove.

Ireland, too, underwent a fantastic witchcraft scandal at this same time. Lady Alice Kyteler, who lived near Kilkenny, had been married to a wealthy banker named William Outlaw, who had died around the year 1300, leaving her a son, William, Junior. Following that, she had three more husbands, each with children of their own. Every new spouse apparently was eager to marry the wealthy widow, but after two had died mysteriously and the third was practically on his death bed, it became painfully evident that she was diverting their wealth, as well as her own, to her son.

This was confirmed by citizens of Kilkenny who noted that on certain evenings, toward twilight, Lady Alice assiduously swept quantities of rubbish from along the street, piling it up in front of her son's door, while she repeated a low chant:

> To the house of William, my son,
> Hie all the wealth of Kilkenny town.

The wealth, meanwhile, hied itself William's way, so Lady Alice was quite properly suspected of using witchcraft to achieve her aims. But charges much more serious than the reciting of a mere doggerel verse were soon leveled in her direction. Her fourth husband, before he succumbed, managed to get hold of various concoctions and implements that she had been using for malevolent purposes and these were turned over to the Bishop of Ossory, who was already looking into the case.

William's money stalled any action by the civil authorities long enough for Lady Alice to escape to England, but a dozen of her subordinates, including William, were rounded up and put on trial. One of Lady Alice's women, named Petronilla, claimed that her mistress had a knowledge of witchcraft unequalled in all the world and proceeded to give the gruesome details.

At Lady Alice's command, Petronilla had frequently sacrificed roosters at a certain crossroads, with the result that a mysterious being invariably appeared, sometimes as a huge cat, other times as a shaggy dog, and occasionally in hideous human guise. His name was Robert Artisson and he not only furnished competent advice in the preparation and casting of spells, but occasionally doubled as Lady Alice's demon lover, visiting her boudoir while Petronilla was present and therefore able to describe the extravagant orgies that transpired.

The most powerful ingredient concocted under the demon's supervision consisted of baneful plants, ground up with squirming worms and mixed with the brains of an unbaptized child in the skull of a robber who had been beheaded. Hair from the heads of executed criminals, nails from dead men's fingers, the entrails of sacrificed animals, also went into various unguents and powders which were used to excite love or hatred, whichever might be preferred in a specific case.

Among the exhibits at the trial was a staff which Lady Alice smeared with a special preparation so that she could ride it like a hobby horse and make her appointed rounds more speedily. From the historic standpoint the staff had a double significance: it represented an early version of the familiar broomsticks on which succeeding generations of countless witches were purported to fly; and it involved a new use for the "flying ointment" that dated from the time of Apuleius and was to figure more and more strongly in the witchcraft of years to come.

The fact that Lady Alice had twelve accomplices is also of historical significance, as it added up to thirteen, the exact number of a coven, or organized group of witches. This has been cited in support of a theory that witch cults were of very ancient origin, although covens, as such, did not come into vogue until a comparatively modern period, as will be discussed later.

The most important aspect of Lady Alice's sordid practices was the invoking of the alleged demon, Robert Artisson, who is still a subject of controversy. Possibly he was a mere human masquerading in a devil's guise to awe such dupes as Petronilla, in which case he probably fled to England along with Lady Alice, to become her fifth husband, since neither was ever heard from again. Conversely, he could have been a fabric of Petronilla's own imagination, if only to crawl out from under the dilemma in which Lady Alice had left her.

Only it didn't work out for Petronilla. She was burned at the stake, along with a few others of the so-called coven. William Outlaw apparently kept much of the loot that his mother had so symbolically raked to his door, except for paying off the civil authorities and putting a new roof on the local cathedral to satisfy the ecclesiastics.

But demonology had gained its foothold. Devil worship and Satanism were on the way up, as opposed to mere wildcat witchcraft. The Establishment of that period depended on the cooperation of state and church to insure civilized progress; so it was logical that persons who rebelled against one would occasionally find allies among those who opposed the other. Civil law treated witchcraft as a crime; ecclesiastic law branded it as heresy. Troubled times were due for witches and their craft in the next few centuries to follow.

4
The Devil's Disciple

Amid the increasing conflict between godliness and deviltry, witchcraft unquestionably attained the ultimate in horror through the machinations of Gilles de Laval, Seigneur de Rais, who at the age of thirty-six completed a career of wanton lust, cruelty and mass murder that stands practically unparalleled. Gilles de Rais, as he was officially known, was not motivated by political hate, vengeance, nor even a fanatical cause. His sole aim was to amass wealth without end by offering the bodies of countless tortured victims as a sacrifice to a Satanic Majesty in whose existence he ardently believed.

Far from outwardly betraying himself as the monster that he was, Gilles de Rais impressed the public as the magnificent seigneur that he was supposed to be. For years, he completely covered his unspeakable excesses; and as both a soldier and a scholar, he rated with the best in France. Craftily, he chose associates who, like himself, were outwardly cultured but inwardly calloused; and his only weakness was the fact that although he was unquestionably the instigator of the hideous ceremonies in which they joined, he naively let them play upon his own gullibility. As a result, he was duped into perpetrating further and unnecessary outrages that they turned into profit for themselves.

Gilles de Laval, later de Rais, was born in the year 1404, in the midst of the period when, as already mentioned, witchcraft was figuring heavily in high places. But important persons who resorted to it were usually seeking to overthrow some existing power; or openly grasping so much wealth that they excited the envy or cupidity of those higher up. At the same time, they were frequently lax in religious observances and therefore reluctant to appear in social circles where their piety might be questioned.

In short, once their ambitions were recognized and feared, they were open to charges of treason by the government, and to charges of heresy by the ecclesiastic councils. Either crime could be charged against anyone using witchcraft, or even countenancing it, which accounted for all the trumped up charges against over-ambition in that period. But Gilles de Rais met the requirements of both state and church, giving each far more than they either demanded or expected. His security lay in the fact that he was obviously ruining himself through reckless squandering and extravagance, which would eventually reduce him to a helpless nonentity. Hence, he was able to pursue the most horrendous career on record, in the foolish belief that it would turn out all the grander.

Born of noble lineage, Gilles was the grandson of a famous knight who inspired him to deeds of valor which, for a time, appeased his wildly sensual nature. Among his vast holdings was the barony of Rais, from which he took his title. When only sixteen, he helped release his overlord, Duke John of Brittany, from rival hands and was rewarded with more lands. At the same age, he married wealthy Katherine of Thouars, whose immense dowry added that much more to his exchecquer.

In 1426, de Rais raised seven companies of soldiers and was assigned to accompany Joan of Arc when she set out to free France from the English. Later, he became a Marshal of France, but by 1432, after the death of his grandfather, he began to retire from military life to enjoy his vast possessions which included the castles of Champtoce, Tiffauges, and many lesser strongholds. Two hundred horsemen accompanied him as a bodyguard and in Orleans, he spent 80,000 crowns in four months, with his retinue taking over all the inns in town.

He produced immense theatrical extravaganzas, all free to the populace, as were the great banquets that followed. But he did not neglect the nobility and clergy. Rather than rouse Duke John's envy by all this pomp, de Rais increased his friendship by selling him choice estates at bargain prices. He gained the good will of John de Malestroit, Bishop of Nantes, by giving vast sums to charity and splendid church rites. De Rais' private chapel was attended by a chapter of thirty canons with choir and service fit for a cathedral.

Apparently, Gilles de Rais was so inculcated with the religious doctrines of the period that he felt capable of choosing between God and the Devil as tangible realities. So he cannily concluded that no matter how much he paid to church and state, the Devil could match and double it, or perhaps triple it, or even quadruple it, if properly evoked. And in a secret sanctum in the dungeon of the Chateau de Tiffauges, de Rais did indeed evoke the Devil. The ruins of these sordid surroundings were vividly described by Montague Summers, one of the most notable modern writers on the subject of witchcraft and demonology:

> At Tiffauges today, from the lonely broken arches of the Chapel, one may pass through a cellar door into the crypt below, which dates from the eleventh century. Of no great size and low-sprung, the solid roof is transversed by heavy, yet not ungraceful, semicircular arches supported by massy pillars whose capitals are relieved with carved lozenges and croziers. The place is gloomy and but a wan, watery daylight seems to filter in, showing the rough broken floor, in one corner of which gapes the naked opening of some oubliette or little well, down which, no doubt, were thrown the dead bodies of the children offered upon the altar-stone.

In such a setting, Gilles de Rais was aided and abetted in his devil worship by two renegade churchmen, Antonio Francesco Prelati and Gilles de Silles. He depended upon several confidential servants to kidnap youthful victims for Satanic sacrifices and also to quash rumors regarding their disappearance. Meanwhile, the hidden crypt was functioning as the center of hideous, sacrilegious rites, which, according to Montague Summers, were probably performed in the following manner:

> *One can well picture the scene illumined only by two black candles, reeking of bitumen and pitch, and by the faint flicker of the rushlight set upon the ground. The silence is broken but by the hoarse blasphemy of the acolyte as he responds in a low tone to the hurried mutter of the young priest clad in the strange vestments of his infernal cult, the mock chasuble of murrey, the hue of dank clotted gore, marked with the inverse cross. The sacred words of power are spoken with a sneer. The golden chalice is raised in hideous parody; the keen knife flashes with swift light; a moment more and the fresh blood gushes into the sacramental cup, from the gaping throat of the youth lying fettered there; poor blood commingles with the saving Blood of God, and as the film of death closes over the agonizing eyes of his victim, Perlatti calls aloud upon Apollyon, the Prince of Darkness, to accept the sacrifice, to manifest and show himself gracious unto his faithful worshippers, granting their desire.*

According to one well-authenticated report, Gilles de Rais made his first great stride toward irrevocable perdition when he inherited another castle containing a library with books written in Latin. These profusely illustrated books related the lives of the early Roman emperors with special emphasis on their vices. After reading and viewing these samples of imperial debauchery, de Rais decided that since he was of equally high estate, he was entitled to similar privileges. But those early emperors were pagans, and thus lost souls regardless of their morals, or lack of them. In contrast, de Rais would be taking a real risk if he emulated them.

So he calculated that risk and took it. So depraved were his desires that he tortured the victims whom he outraged and gloated as he watched their death agonies. According to some estimates, their number ran into the hundreds, for the greater and more wanton the slaughter, the more de Rais proved himself a true disciple of the Devil, whom he was ready to accept as master.

To that end, de Rais wrote out pacts in his own blood, and he was said to have used the blood of many victims to inscribe red-lettered pages of conjurations calculated to bring the Devil himself.

De Rais actually counted on the Devil to provide him with needed riches, and to that end he reserved the choicest victims of his lust as human sacrifices on the Satanic altar where Prelati, de Silles, and other specialists in evil, performed their diabolical rites. They not only went along with whatever de Rais wanted; they tended to increase the tempo of his monstrous urges, for as Gilles' financial status reached a precarious stage, the greater their priority became.

Fundamental to all this was the fact that de Rais retained the right to buy back any of the holdings that he was selling off so cheaply to Duke John and others. Always, he was anticipating vast wealth to arrive from infernal sources overnight; but finally, he was willing to settle for anything. The main reason why de Rais had chosen Prelati to conduct the diabolical rites was because the renegade supposedly had a familiar demon of his own, called Barron, whom he could summon almost at will. So de Rais ordered Prelati to evoke his familiar and let Barron listen to a request for gold that de Rais would make in person.

Prelati went through all the required formalities, but Barron failed to appear while Gilles de Rais was around, so Prelati promised to summon the familiar privately and put in the request himself. He did so and came to de Rais with the enthusiastic report that Barron had delivered a quantity of gold ingots that were stacked about Prelati's apartment; but, in accordance with demoniac procedure, they were to be left untouched for a specified number of days.

Gilles de Rais tried to wait it out, but couldn't. He ordered Prelati to unlock the apartment before the appointed time. The door, when opened, revealed the golden glitter that de Rais had hoped to see, but moments later, Prelati, who had entered first, came rushing out, warning de Rais back and barring the door from the outside, just in time. Prelati, it seemed, had practically stumbled over a huge green serpent that Barron had installed as guardian of the gold; and he had almost fallen prey to its deadly fangs.

De Rais wanted to enter the apartment with a crucifix to drive away the serpent, but Prelati warned him that it might cause Barron to stay away as well. So they waited until the stipulated day and found that the guardian serpent was gone, but that the gold ingots had been turned to tinsel, which crumpled under touch. But gullible Gilles, far from suspecting that Barron was a product of Prelati's fertile imagination, kept begging the renegade to let him sign blood pacts pledging direct obedience to the demon in return for gold that would remain real long enough for him to pay off his most pressing debts.

Prelati insisted that Barron would first have to be reconciled by a major sacrifice, so de Rais supplied a glass receptacle containing a child's heart, hands, eyes and blood as a special offering to the offended demon. Further rituals followed on a more gruesome scale than ever, but before Barron could be sufficiently appeased to deliver, Gilles de Rais came to the end of his rope; not just figuratively, but literally as well.

Gilles' wife had left him soon after he had launched on his monstrous career and the disappearance of so many children from the neighborhood of his various castles during half a dozen years had excited increasing rumors. Finally, one of his confidants, who had not been taken into his diabolical rites, became suspicious and fled from the Castle of Tiffauges.

Thus a case was building up against de Rais when he made the mistake of using force to take back a castle he had sold to Duke John's treasurer. This caused the rift that the duke had long awaited and Gilles de Rais was soon brought to trial, both in ecclesiastical and civil courts, where a formidable list of forty-nine counts was brought against him. As more and more evidence was produced, de Rais lost his haughty composure and admitted his guilt. Then, after two of his servants testified that they had counted the heads of nearly fifty children as his victims and followed with first-hand descriptions of his orgies, de Rais, under threat of torture, made what was claimed to be a full confession.

Brought before his judges, he added abundant details of his atrocities, graphically reenacting his sadistic outrages and gloatingly recalling his monstrous motivations. According to accounts, his listeners sat in stunned silence while de Rais completed his tale; then, reversing his manner entirely, he delivered an impassioned plea to the parents of those he had so cruelly slain, begging them to forgive him and pray for him.

Though sentenced to be burned for his crimes, Gilles de Rais was first hanged; then his body was dropped from the gibbet into the flames, from where it was promptly reclaimed by his relatives and given an honorable burial. Apparently he died in the firm belief that his gruesome confession had expiated all his crimes and sins, which had at least a touch of warped logic, considering that the Devil had totally rejected his overtures and refused him aid that he should have rightfully or wrongfully received.

But the populace thought differently. During the centuries that followed, the children of Brittany were taught never to loiter around castle gates nor follow in the wake of an elegant parade of cavalry. Legend related how Gilles de Rais had originally worn a ruddy beard, but year by year, its redness gradually disappeared, until of all things, it finally turned blue, which could only have happened if all the blood had been drained from it — by the Devil.

From that conjecture developed the fanciful tale of Bluebeard, a very tame character compared to his prototype, Gilles de Rais. All that Bluebeard did was chop off the heads of seven wives, who by his standards, may have properly deserved it for letting their curiosity get the better of them and looking into a room which each had been instructed never to unlock. But it was a tale good enough to frighten children far from Brittany through many successive generations and discourage them from prying into places where they had no right to go.

The case of Gilles de Rais stands as a landmark in the annals of witchcraft because it shows the fantastic limits to which such beliefs could go. Whether or not all the charges against him were true is open to debate, but the people who accepted them as fact began to wonder, not why Gilles de Rais had done what he had, but why he hadn't gotten away with it. The courts that convicted de Rais did not dismiss the Devil as non-existent, for if they had, they might have had to declare de Rais innocent. So the net result was twofold:

People in high places didn't blame the Devil for not coming to the aid of Gilles de Rais; they blamed Gilles de Rais. Maybe he had used the wrong approach, squandering his money on the Devil, who didn't need it. Maybe they could do better in a more subtle way, particularly if they dealt more sharply with the in-between operators, like Prelati and de Silles, so they did.

Those of lesser personage, however, were in their heyday. Every creepy little witch or warlock who was trying to invoke the Devil's aid, but couldn't, due to lack of finances, now was sure that finance wasn't needed.

As for Gilles de Rais, this much might be said in his behalf, even though he in no way deserved it: For the dozens, and perhaps hundreds, that he wantonly sacrificed to witchcraft, there were to be not only hundreds, but thousands, and, by some estimates, hundreds of thousands sacrificed for the same reason. Maybe Gilles de Rais triggered it; maybe he didn't. Anyway, it happened.

5
Witchcraft on the Wing

Among the ancient myths that carried over to the Middle Ages was that of a skyland called Magonia, whose inhabitants sent fleets of ships disguised as clouds to plague the people of this earth. Very probably, the shapes of certain clouds suggested mammoth sailing ships, while the way in which low clouds scudded swiftly before a heavy wind seemed further proof that they were bound upon some monstrous mission. But the final and most convincing touch was supplied by hailstorms, which were plausibly attributed to the Magonians dumping cargoes overboard, obviously with malice aforethought, because they not only damaged crops, but drove people to shelter, so that it was impossible for people to protect their fields. This led to the belief that the cloudmen landed their ships at the finish of such storms, loaded the crops that the hailstones had beaten down, and took off again for Magonia, greatly enriched at the expense of the poor earthly peasants, who were left to reap the pitiful remnants of their devastated harvests.

This fitted the pattern of ancient pirate raids along the shores of the Mediterranean Sea, as well as later ravages of the Vikings and the Norsemen on the coasts of England and France. Just as such invasions were often aided by spies who signalled from land, so did the Magonians depend upon treacherous earthly folk. Their raids were blamed on a special class of witches known as Tempestarii, who actually raised the storms that brought the ruthless cloudmen.

Fleecy clouds, drifting over the ripening fields, were cover for Magonian scout ships, picking up signals from the ground below. Flashes of lightning, rumbles of thunder and especially chill winds that preceded hailstorms, were proof that the Tempestarii were at work. After the damage was done, the outraged peasants, looking up to the sky, not only saw long rakish clouds that represented departing Magonian ships; sometimes they spotted stray, scudding wisps that resembled human shapes. Those, of course, were the Tempestarii, chasing after the Magonians to collect their fees, fitting the notion of witches flying into the sky.

As a result, the peasantry was easily bamboozled by a special class of practitioners who claimed they could nullify the machinations of the Tempestarii, but demanded a share of the undamaged crops in return. Thus the ancient art of witchcraft merged with the coming science of insurance. Unfortunately, these practitioners lacked the modern devices so necessary to their trade — statistics and computers. When they guessed wrong, which was often, they attributed it to increased activity by the Tempestarii and a witch-hunt was apt to follow.

Charles Godfrey Leland (1824–1903), noted student of European folklore and gypsy sorcery, has traced the Magonia legend back to the ancient Etruscans (about 600 B.C. or before), basing his findings on the survival of such myths among the natives of modern Tuscany. Other scholars, however, have found similar legends throughout the Orient, notably in Japan, and amid the Mayan lore of Mexico and Central America.

Around the year 820, Agobard, Bishop of Lyons, rescued three men and a woman from a mob that was about to stone them to death, thinking that they were Magonians who had fallen from one of their cloud ships. More probably they were stray members from a band of roving gypsies. Agobard also denounced other superstitions prevalent in his time, but to little avail. They continued to spread and the Magonian legend was confirmed four centuries later by a historical writer, Gervase of Tilbury, who told how one of their ships dropped an anchor from a low cloud, only to have it hook so firmly in a mound of earth that they could not free it.

Thereupon a sailor came down the rope, but before he could release the anchor, he slumped to the ground, gasping from the increased air pressure. Some people arrived and started pulling the rope downward and the Magonians, hearing the shouts from below, cut the rope and took off through the clouds, abandoning their comrade to his fate. He soon died from the crushing force of air pressure upon his chest and was buried with due ceremony, while the anchor was mounted over the door of the local church as proof positive that the Magonians had been there.

Oddly, this account may have had some bearing on modern talk of flying saucers and mysterious space ships, a phenomena which can be traced back through the centuries. Maybe the Unidentified Flying Objects (UFO's) of today were the things that they reported then. Whether they were or not, is something that does not matter. That people will believe in anything, no matter how absurd, is an axiom, or self-evident truth that does not have to be proven.

Since witches could raise tempests at command, they naturally could perform other wonders, such as damaging property, killing animals or people, causing injuries, sickness, love, hate, in fact about anything they wanted, especially if it happened to be baleful. This demanded a cooperative effort on the part of witches, including the instruction of new recruits, the exchange of trade secrets, and above all, worship of the Devil as grand master of the entire show. Hence, by the time such aristocratic Satanists as Gilles de Rais were invoking His Mephistophelean Majesty with bloody rites in secret crypts, witches of the commoner sort were allegedly assembling in vast conclaves for the same insidious purpose.

This was by no means a mere reversion to the almost totally forgotten Diana cult in a new guise of devil worship, though a few off-trail authorities are inclined to such opinion. Other factors were definitely involved and loomed to greater proportions as time went on. Almost from its beginning, the Christian Church was confronted by one heresy after another, the term "heresy" meaning "a religious error held in willful and persistent opposition to the truth after it has been defined and declared by the Church in an authoritative manner."

Before the year 400 or so, the heretical trend was to inject pagan elements into the Christian faith, so a recurrence of Diana worship would have been understandable. But by that time, the Church had attained a distinctive character that rendered it virtually immune to such inroads. In later centuries, the situation changed. Then, many of the heresies became differences in the interpretation of Christian truths, which, according to one school of thought, did not really threaten the very life of the Church.

Others, however, saw a new and greater menace from such sects as the Cathars, or Cathari, who flourished from A.D. 900–1300. These worshippers attributed so much earthly power to Satan that they came to regard him as almost the equal of God in heaven. Hence the Cathari were charged with a dualistic form of worship and were accordingly branded as heretics. Wholesale suppression of such groups caused their scattered remnants to go underground and become still more virulent; while other sects arose who finally went all-out for devil worship.

About the year 1350, one cult, the Luciferians, were accused of catering to demons with rites as foul as they were fiendish. Their infernal ceremonies, according to confessions that some allegedly made to their inquisitors, read like something out of modern fantasy fiction. Possibly, when questioned, they tried to cover up their actual activities with fabrications that they thought were too ridiculous to be believed; yet they were. Or possibly, they remained so sullenly silent that their interrogators simply wrote their own imaginary accounts, confident that people generally would believe anything, which, in those times, they did.

Until that period, witchcraft, though denounced and punishable in various ways, had seldom evoked severe penalties from civil and ecclesiastical courts. But witchcraft was apparently on the increase, if only because more people were on the watch for it, so the obvious conclusion was that many cases were probably the outcrop of the underground activities of the suppressed heretic sects. There was one sure way to counteract that; namely, to denounce witchcraft itself as a form of heresy and treat it just as rigorously.

During the three hundred years between 1450 and 1750, death at the stake was the common mode of dealing with heretics in Europe, and as it was believed that most witches were heretical in their views, witch-burning followed as a logical matter of course.

Actually, as we have already seen, witchcraft was surging to the fore in all its Satanic fury, prior to 1450, as witness the case of Gilles de Rais; and it was to carry over long after the year 1750, indeed into the world of today. But those three centuries represent the Great Witch Delusion in all its fiery fury. So widespread was the mania that no exact figures can be compiled as to the extent of its ravages, but conservative estimates run to about 200,000 victims, half of those in Germany alone, although others claim that the total may have run into millions.

So ardent was the urge to stamp out witchcraft that any trumped up charge was sufficient to bring an unfortunate victim to trial. Equally great were the efforts to tie in individual witches with groups ranging in size from local covens to massed assemblages, in order to prove the added crime of devil worship. Decrepit hags were frequently accused of witchery by spiteful neighbors and, since they were often too infirm to hobble to the alleged witch meetings, they were credited with riding broomsticks or fiends disguised as animals in order to reach their goal. That rather unorthodox manner of transportation gave them unlimited range, but still allowed them an alibi if they were never seen to leave the hovels where they dwelt; so to offset that, imaginary flights were accepted as realities. Anyone seen and recognized as a participant in a diabolical conclave, had no course but to admit having been there, which, in turn, meant naming others who were present. During the years, such accounts increased in number because the interrogators found new and more terrifying instruments of torture for squeezing confessions from the persons they accused.

Germany was a special target of such campaigns, primarily because it had been a hotbed for so many rebellious outlanders who had indulged in diabolical rites. Some of those groups may have done no more than mock the solemn pomp of the Church, which the rebels felt was allied with the feudal barons who tried to rule them; while others might have represented outright Satanism. Either way, the fact that they persisted in secret was proof that the Devil had really taken over; hence the continued reports of vast assemblages of witches and their accompanying fiends on the summit of the Brocken.

Such a rendezvous was styled a *sabbat*, or witches' sabbath, and the Brocken was the reputed scene of an annual convention of international proportions, which brought witches from all parts of Europe to celebrate Walpurgis Night, the eve before May Day. Regional meetings were also held there and at certain high, forbidding summits, bearing the common title of Blocksburg, in countries other than Germany.

But lofty heights were not always needed for the grand sabbats, as the more important events were known. In Brittany, witches were supposed to meet among the ancient cromlechs of that land, which like the ruins of Stonehenge are of Druid origin. In England, open commons served as meeting spots, though the witches sometimes preferred the depths of forest glades, where the Devil would obligingly appear to them at high noon. In the Channel Islands, between England and France, witches chose open beaches or the shelter of high rocks; but either formed convenient lookouts from which they could combine their efforts to produce sudden and unexpected storms to wreck the fishing fleets plying in those waters.

Lesser sabbats were held in any handy place that people habitually shunned at night, such as a remote crossroad, a cemetery, a ravine, a ruined church or a supposedly haunted house. They were held weekly, originally on Thursdays, which through some form of rationalization, was regarded as neutral; but sooner or later, the Devil was allowed his due on Mondays, Wednesdays and Fridays. That raised the question: Why shouldn't he have them all? So he was granted any day, which meant that every day could be Devil's day, where witches were involved.

The approximate data of 1450 is significant, as it represents one of the earliest mentions of the witches' sabbat. The link with the night riders who worshipped Diana is quite evident, along with Norse and other legends, including that of Magonia. The "flying ointment," as the mixture used by witches for aerial transportation came to be called, can be traced back to the time of Apuleius. The emergence of such old ideas in the new guise of devil worship simply served to mark witchcraft as a heinous crime indeed.

The pattern was set for things to come. As fast as witches were brought to trial, they were questioned regarding their attendance at their secret conclaves and the wilder they let their imagination run, the more their inquisitors embroidered upon it. On the contrary, if they minimized their descriptions, or truthfully detailed the stupid get-togethers of local malcontents who had nothing to gain and everything to lose, their confessions were reduced to the most sordid terms. Instead of feasting on rich delicacies, as described at so many sabbats, they were presumably compelled to dine on pie baked from disinterred corpses, garnished plentifully with garbage.

On at least one occasion, the choicest delicacies were replaced with rancid, stinking fare and the finest wines were supplanted by a thick, unsavory liquid that looked, smelled and tasted like blood, because it was blood. Yet the participants were supposed to enjoy such banquets; and what was more, they did. Acceptance of such ghoulish provender was the sure way to establish oneself as a Grade-A witch.

Such ideas did not spring full-blown in the year 1450. Rather, they were the result of slow, but steady evolution during the next thirty-five or forty years, when they were forged, tempered and finally struck into the most powerful weapon of their day — the *Malleus Maleficarum*, or "Hammer of the Witches," as it was appropriately termed. This was a literary work penned by a pair of highly able, but much less amiable, authors, who set a pace for persecution that persisted for the next few centuries.

So strong were the strokes of that hammer, both theoretically and theologically, that the *Malleus Maleficarum* deserves a chapter of its own.

6
The Hammer of the Witches

Don't think that witchcraft had an easy time establishing itself as Satan's Number One Secret Weapon, back in the year 1450. It had a very active and endurable rival for that claim in the form of a new and utterly fantastic mechanical device that could only have been concocted by the Devil himself, with all of Hell's minions standing by to help. That thing, which was horrible then and may still be far more horrible today, was a contraption called the printing press.

Until then, books were produced by scribes who laboriously copied them by hand. The mere thought of stamping them out by the hundreds was harder to believe than tales of the witches' sabbat, so it was not surprising that an ignorant and superstitious public would put them in the same category. Witches supposedly had helpers known as "familiars" who were actually demons disguised as animals or other creatures; and that could be why an apprentice in a print shop came to be called a "printer's devil."

Among early examples of the power of the press were certain books attacking and denouncing witchcraft in all its virulent forms. These circulated far wider, faster, and in much greater number than the old handwritten manuscripts. The *Malleus Maleficarum* was the most important and most popular of these works. Appearing first in 1486, it summed all the known facts and fancies then current regarding witchcraft, handling the subject in such scholarly and authoritative style that it became a manual for witch hunters from then on.

This book was published in dozens of editions in Latin, German, French, Italian and finally English versions, retaining its superior status over a period of two centuries. It was written by two of the most learned men of their day, Jakob Sprenger, Dean of Cologne University, and Prior Heinrich Kramer. Both were inquisitors who had been granted special powers to suppress witchcraft in Northern Germany, where such enormities and abominations had been notoriously rampant due to the laxity and even the possible connivance of some of the local magistrates. So Sprenger and Kramer spelled it all out in *Malleus Maleficarum*, or *Hexenhammer*. The book covered all phases of witchcraft, including the identification of culprits and every stage of procedure to be taken against them.

Modern opinions regarding *Malleus Maleficarum* are varied indeed. It has been classed as "a very great and very wise book" rating as "the most prominent, the most important, the most authoritative volume in the whole vast literature of witchcraft," and that "from the point of psychology, from the point of jurisprudence, from the point of history, it is supreme."

Other reviewers, while in agreement regarding its importance, are less enthusiastic as to the other claims. One terms the *Malleus Maleficarum* "the most portentous monument of superstition which the world has produced" and defines Sprenger, its chief author, as "a man of the most dangerous type, an honest fanatic." Another critic regards it as "without question, the most important and most sinister work on demonology ever written," largely on the ground that it "opened the floodgates of inquisitorial hysteria."

Still other opinions categorize *Malleus Maleficarum* as "a notorious work," or "an enormously interesting and disturbing work," or "one of the most appalling books that has ever been written," or simply "the terrible *Malleus Maleficarum*." Other critiques are directed more at its context, thereby echoing a summarization which Sir Walter Scott once applied to witchcraft trials in general, namely that "the mode of judicial procedure against witches, and the nature of the evidence admissible, opened a door to accusers and left the accused no chance of escape."

So the best course is to consider the general contents of the highly disputed *Malleus Maleficarum* and follow with some pointed excerpts from this great-grandaddy of all treatises on witchcraft and let the material speak for itself. Merely remember that it represents propositions that were established about 1480 or perhaps much earlier, but that they carried through almost to modern times and are still accepted in some remote localities today.

The great work is divided into three parts, the first dealing with what the authors regard as the three necessary concomitants of witchcraft — the Devil, a witch and the permission of Almighty God. This is subdivided into lesser parts, covering many phases of witchcraft as accepted at the time, but giving final opinions in cases where there might be any doubt. In so doing, the authors assiduously demolished the arguments of any persons who disagreed with them on even the finest points, thereby setting themselves up as final authorities for all time.

The second part treats the evils wrought by witches and gives instructions on how they may be nullified or neutralized. This consists of two general sections, one covering the operations of the witches themselves; the other, remedies for persons who have been bewitched, as well as counteractive measures against those employed by witches. Each of these parts is divided into lesser sections or chapters.

The third part, which may have been chiefly the work of Kramer, concerns the judicial proceedings as held in both ecclesiastical and civil courts, not only against witches but all heretics as well. However, the emphasis, as would naturally be expected, is heavily on witchcraft, as that was the menace Sprenger and Kramer were assigned to combat. The broader coverage is a tribute to the workings of their keen judicial minds, since they left not the slightest loophole in any procedure they advised.

This third part has three heads: The first deals with such matters as initiating proceedings, the number of witnesses and who may qualify as such. The second goes into matters of the trial, whether a witch is to be imprisoned and the manner of taking her, the appointment of an advocate for the defence, and finally the questioning of the suspect, along with the application of tortures. The third head covers the kinds of sentences, determined by the type and degree of witchcraft involved.

To do even a chapter outline of *Malleus Maleficarum* would be difficult indeed, for the book is a large one, containing some eighty chapters, or questions, as some of them are termed, and it runs to a total of nearly a quarter-million words. Much of this would also be superfluous where modern readers are concerned, because Sprenger and Kramer were master hands at building up long-winded arguments and theories just for the fun of knocking them down in equally verbose style.

This is no reflection on their ability. Quite to the contrary, they treated the subject skillfully and systematically, apparently proving to their own satisfaction that witches can change themselves into animals and accomplish other wonders with Satan's aid. They speak convincingly of dangers to which they personally were exposed; and they quote witnesses of seemingly unimpeachable character to back up their findings.

Dr. Henry Charles Lea (1825-1909) spent a long lifetime researching and writing about church history in the Middle Ages. Of Sprenger, in particular, Dr. Lea stated:

> *All his vast experience and wide erudition are brought to the task of proving the reality of witchcraft and the extent of its evils; and further, of instructing the inquisitor how to elude the wiles of Satan and to punish his devotees. He was no vulgar witch finder, but a man trained in all the learning of the schools. He apparently was not inhumane. In many places he manifests a laudable desire to give the accused the benefit of whatever pleas they might rightfully put forward, but he is so fully convinced of the gigantic character of the evils to be combated, he so thoroughly believes that his tribunal is engaged in a contest with Satan for human souls, that he eagerly justifies every artifice and every cruelty that could be suggested to outwit the adversary on whom fair play would be thrown away.*

Like Dr. Lea, another noted writer on witchcraft, Dr. Charles Mackay (1814–1889) saw the dangers that developed from the regular form of trial specified in *Malleus Maleficarum*. Mackay, elaborating on the previously quoted pithy comment of Sir Walter Scott, had this to say regarding the results of the methods recommended in the *Hexenhammer:*

> *The questions, which were always enforced by torture, were of the most absurd and disgusting nature. The inquisitors were required to ask the suspected:*
> *Whether they had midnight meetings with the Devil?*
> *Whether they attended the witches' sabbath on the Brocken?*
> *Whether they had familiar spirits?*
> *Whether they could raise whirlwinds and call down the lightning?*
> *Whether they had sexual intercourse with Satan?*
> *The great resemblance between the confessions of the unhappy victims was regarded as a new proof of the existence of the crime. But this is not astonishing. The same questions from the* Malleus Maleficarum *were put to them all and torture never failed to educe*

> the answer required by the inquisitor. *Numbers of people, whose imaginations were filled with these horrors, went further in the way of confession than even their tormentors anticipated, in the hope that they would thereby be saved from the rack and put out of their misery at once.*

Between them Drs. Lea and Mackay gave little consideration to the arguments advanced by Drs. Sprenger and Kramer, treating them as sheer fanaticism. But the authors of *Malleus Maleficarum* had plenty to say for themselves in their own book:

> *The judge may punish her (the accused witch) with imprisonment with the following object in view. Let him summon her friends to say that she may escape the death penalty ... if she confesses the truth and urge them to persuade her to do so. We have found that witches have been so strengthened by this advice that they have spat on the ground as if in the Devil's face, saying, "Depart, cursed Devil! I shall do what is just!" and afterwards, they have confessed their crimes.*

After that, who wouldn't have? Probably even Dr. Lea and Dr. Mackay would have confessed them, four centuries later, if they'd had any crimes to confess. But let's go back to 1486:

> *But if, after keeping the accused in suspense, while continually postponing the day of questioning and using other persuasions, the judge should be sure that the accused is denying the truth, let him question her lightly, to confess the truth voluntarily; if she will not, let him order the officers to bind her to some engine of torture and let them obey at once, but not joyfully, rather appearing to be disturbed by their duty.*
>
> *Then let her be released again at someone's earnest request and taken on one side; and let her again be persuaded; and in persuading her, let her be told that she can escape the death penalty.*

That sounds like a trick used in the modern third degree, where the police let up after an intensive questioning and a kindly old officer coaxes a confession from an unwary young crook by promising to let him off lightly if he tells all he knows. In underworld parlance, such a character is called a "Mother Bull"; what the term was back around 1480, Sprenger and Kramer did not specify.

However, they did raise the question of whether it was lawful for a judge to promise the accused her life, in a case where only her confession is needed for her to receive the death sentence.

There, the authors were cagey about speaking for themselves. Instead, they gave opinions existing at the time, one being that if the accused should be a notoriously bad witch and the mistress of other witches, she could be sentenced to life imprisonment on bread and water, provided that she supply evidence leading to the conviction of other witches. The authors hastened to add — and this of their own volition — that the accused should never be told that she was to be imprisoned as described; rather, she should be led to believe that some lesser penalty, such as exile, would be imposed upon her.

Through the opinions of others, the authors blandly point out that some feel that after a witch has been imprisoned in this way, the promise to spare her life should be kept for a specific period, but after that, she should be burned. There was a third opinion, however, that was preferable: the judge could safely promise the accused her life, but in such a manner that he might later disclaim the duty of passing the actual sentence, by delegating that function to some other judge, who presumably would know nothing of the promise, though the authors avoided any mention of that point.

So far, no actual torture was involved, but the same chapter recommended its application when neither threats nor promises could induce a suspected witch to confess. They advised:

While she is being questioned on each point, she should be frequently exposed to torture, beginning with the gentler sort and that there should be no haste in employing graver methods. Meanwhile, the notary should write down all the questions and answers, as well as the modes of torture.

If she confesses under torture, she should be taken elsewhere and questioned again, so that her answers can be recorded as voluntary. If she does not confess under the usual torture, the judge should have other instruments of torture brought in and shown to her, so he can tell her that she will have to endure those if she does not confess.

All this and much, much more from *Malleus Maleficarum* explains why later writers like Scott and Mackay were not at all amazed by the consistency of the answers given by suspected witches, no matter how outlandish the questions. Whenever judges referred faithfully to the *Hexenhammer*, which many judges did during the next few centuries, they were sure to come up with stereotyped reports.

A striking feature of *Malleus Maleficarum* is its blend of advanced psychology with outworn superstition. The authors — probably Sprenger, in particular — were far ahead of their time with certain ideas, yet always ready to fall back on any old, established beliefs that helped to solidify their opinions. They recognized that unrestrained imagination could cause a variety of illusions and might thereby influence a man's sensations, or "sensible powers" as they termed them; and from there they went on to say:

> *Such a power of imagination can change adjacent bodies, so that a man may walk along a narrow plank down the middle of a street; but if the plank were suspended over deep water, he would not dare to walk along it, because his imagination would impress upon his mind the idea of falling; therefore his body and the power of his limbs would obey his imagination.*
>
> *This change may be compared to the influence exercised by the eyes of a person who has such influence and so a mental change is brought about although there is no actual bodily change.*

That was talking in terms of autosuggestion and hypnotism three or four centuries before such things were really understood; but the authors, true to form, proceeded to make other analogies that they turned into false conclusions:

> *If it be argued that such a change is caused by a living body, due to the influence of the mind upon some other living body, this answer may be given: In the presence of a murderer, blood flows from the corpse of the person he has slain. Therefore, without any mental powers, bodies can produce wonderful effects; so a living man, if he pass by the corpse of a murdered man, although unaware of the dead body, is often seized with fear.*
>
> *There are also some things in nature which have certain hidden*

powers, the reason for which no one knows. Such for example is the lodestone, which attracts iron and steel.

So do women bring about changes in the bodies of others by making use of certain things which are beyond our knowledge, but this is done without aid from the Devil. But because these remedies are mysterious, we can not attribute them to the Devil, as we would attribute evil spells cast by witches.

Moreover, witches use certain images and other amulets which they place under the doorways of houses, or in meadows where animals are herded, or even where men gather; and thus they cast spells over their victims, who have often been known to die.

Many case histories are cited in *Malleus Maleficarum* to illustrate the ways and wiles of witches, some drawn from older sources, others from the testimony of supposedly reliable witnesses, and still more from the observations or experiences of the authors themselves. On one occasion, Sprenger and Kramer were hastily summoned to investigate a violent hailstorm near Salzburg, where all the fruit, crops and vineyards had been destroyed in a belt one mile wide. After some deliberation, the inquisitors decided it to be a case of witchcraft and rounded up all likely suspects.

Among these were two women named Agnes and Anna, who apparently were not only crones but cronies, so the judges questioned them separately. Agnes gave way under threat of torture and confessed that for eighteen years she had lived in sin with an incubus and that on the day of the storm, a familiar had come to her and told her to take a bowl of water to a field outside the town gate. There, Agnes found the Devil standing opposite a tower. At his direction, she dug a hole, poured the water into it and stirred it with her finger.

Thereupon, the Devil carried the water up into the air, turning it into the hailstorm, which he obligingly delayed just long enough for Agnes to get back to the shelter of her house. Amazed that one witch could have accomplished all that, the judges asked Agnes if she had an accomplice and she promptly named Anna, saying that she had seen her beneath a tree opposite, but did not know what she was doing there.

The judges put the same questions to Anna, but found her reluctant to answer them until she was lifted up by her thumbs, so she was just clear of the ground. Once released from that mild torture, Anna admitted that she, too, had stirred up water at the Devil's instigation and she corroborated all the statements that Agnes had made. They were both burned the next day.

Agnes commended herself to God, saying she would die with a willing heart to escape the tortures of the Devil, but Anna scoffed at her for that. The judges, thorough as usual, checked into Anna's refusal to repent and found that she had been living with an incubus for a full twenty years and had done far more harm to men, cattle and crops, then Agnes had.

The most powerful class of witches, according to *Malleus Maleficarum* consists of those who, against every instinct of human nature, are in the habit of devouring the children of their own species. In addition to raising hailstorms, tempests and lightning, as well as causing sterility in men and animals, they offer to devils the children whom they do not devour. These monstrous creatures could also throw children into streams when no one was in sight; make horses go mad under their riders; they were able to transport themselves from one place to another, either in body or in imagination; they could prevent judges from deciding against them; they could keep silent under torture and cause others to do the same; they could turn minds to love or hatred; they were able to bewitch animals or men with a mere glance; and they had the power to see distant things as though they were present, as well as foretelling the future.

As part of their pact with the Devil, such witches often brought somewhat less capable novices to him for initiation into the cult, thus greatly increasing the number of witches. When Sprenger and Kramer questioned a young girl in a town near Basle, she told them that she had often been transported by night with her aunt over great distances, sometimes as far as from Strasbourg to Cologne.

When asked whether they could be transported only in imagination or actually in the body, she replied that it was possible both ways. Flying ointment was often needed to make a trip in person, but the devils, if properly called upon, would supply a bluish vapor through which the distant meeting could be viewed as clearly as if the witch had traveled to the scene. Unfortunately, the young witch's aunt could not be brought in to corroborate this testimony, because the law had caught up with her in Strasbourg and she had been burned there.

Other cases of transvection, or aerial flight, were also cited in *Malleus Maleficarum* to prove that the Devil could transport people bodily, either by an invisible force, or by providing strange creatures to carry them through the air. Those creatures were actually lesser demons in disguise, tying in with the common belief in "familiars."

The authors of *Malleus Maleficarum* went into explicit details involving a case of witchcraft in a town near Strasbourg, where a workman was chopping wood when three large cats sprang upon him in quick succession, clawing him furiously. He managed to drive them off by beating one on the head, another on the back and the third on the legs. An hour later, two officers arrived and forced the workman to accompany them to a magistrate, who summarily threw him in jail without a hearing.

Three days later, he was tried on the charge of having entered a wealthy home and beaten three respectable matrons of the town so soundly that they were still incapacitated. The workman was able to prove, however, that he could not have left his premises long enough to be culpable, so when he told about the cats, the amazed magistrates decided that it must have been the work of the Devil.

In analyzing this, Sprenger and Kramer took the attitude that the three women were witches who were transformed into cats at the Devil's instigation. Perhaps the most regrettable feature of this case was that the magistrates apparently were too faint-hearted to charge the wealthy matrons with witchcraft, even with all the indisputable logic of the Sprenger-Kramer team at their disposal.

Bewitchment of cattle is also covered in *Malleus Maleficarum*. One popular method is described as follows: The witch places a milking stool and pail in a corner of her house and sticks a knife at an angle in the wall above it. She then calls upon her familiar and tells him that she wants the milk from some neighbor's cow. While the Devil takes the milk from the cow, the witch acts as though milking the knife and the actual milk flows from the knife into the pail.

Such practices could carry an insidious aftermath, according to *Malleus Maleficarum*, which states that many women whose cows have been deprived of milk have consulted with suspected witches and have received remedies from them, but only by giving some small favor in return. Such favors were invariably of an irreverent or sacrilegious sort, thus paving the way toward the personal perdition of anyone who acquiesced.

In all, *Malleus Maleficarum* is a most illuminating work, deserving of all that has been said of it; and more, much more. To class it as the "Hammer of the Witches," is mild, indeed. The term "sledgehammer" would have been more appropriate, for it left its impact not only upon its own generation, but upon many more to follow. So the proper process is to keep its priceless precepts constantly in mind, as we move onward to our more — or less — enlightened era.

7
The Call Goes Out

For a full century following the appearance of *Malleus Maleficarum*, witches were both prosecuted and persecuted with increasing severity along the established lines. New territories were often opened more rapidly than witchcraft could be stamped out in old, hence the craze was constantly on the rise. Add to that the zeal of new witch hunters who were naturally eager to outdo their predecessors and the results were just about what should have been expected.

Where Sprenger and Kramer had been inclined to show fair play toward persons accused of witchcraft on the evidence of a lone witness, or sometimes no more than two, later writers felt that such a limitation was like playing into the hands of the Devil himself. What was more, they cited cases to prove their point, such as those attributed to Bartolomeo de Spina, whose book on witchcraft appeared in the year 1523.

One case involved a man who was discovered drunk in a ducal wine cellar and would probably have been accused of attempted robbery if he hadn't come up with a more plausible story. He claimed that he had seen his wife preparing for a witches' sabbat, so he had copied her procedure to find out where she went. He had landed amid the witches in the wine cellar, so alarming them that they had taken off in a body. Unable to find his way from the cellar, he had been drinking to drown his fear of their return. The poor man was cleared of theft and his wife was burned as the witch she must have been.

The other instance concerned an innocent young girl from Bergamo, who was surprised in the bed of a married man in Venice. Her only mistake had been watching her mother smear herself with flying ointment and, seeing how well it worked, she had done the same. Her flight landed her in the house in Venice where her mother was about to murder the man's child, but flew off when she realized she was discovered. They burned the girl's mother.

Considering the ease with which de Spina could shunt the blame on witches, it is not surprising that he and his associates were credited with burning at least a hundred witches in the area of Como during that same year, 1523; and that he estimated that during the next year, one thousand were burned throughout Northern Italy.

To say that witch burning was spreading like wildfire through

France at this period would be putting it almost literally, for according to one authority, fires for the execution of witches blazed in almost every town. In Piedmont, so many witches were said to have been burned that, in one township, every family lost at least one member. Any rebellions that did break out were the exceptions rather than the rule, because the people were so steeped in ignorance and superstition that the closer witchcraft came to home, the more real it seemed.

In addition to relaxing the laws on witnesses, new types of testimony were allowed, all to the discomfort of suspected witches. New and improved modes of torture were introduced, so that the "gentler" sort once recommended in *Malleus Maleficarum* became nonexistent. Preliminary forms of torture were apparently introduced as mere routine prior to the initial questioning of a suspect, but no mention was made of it in the records, so the confessions were classed as voluntary.

Another point on which Sprenger and Kramer had been sticklers, namely the appointment of an advocate for the defense, was overruled by the more ardent witch hunters. To side with a suspect could mean becoming the Devil's advocate as well, since he was the only witness upon whom a witch would really rely. That explained, too, why one member of a family would turn against another, just for safety's sake.

An account of one French trial tells how a group of women, including a few who were young and beautiful, were accused of having joined a witches' dance at midnight under a blasted oak, where they had been recognized by creditable people. The husbands of the women insisted that, at the time specified, their wives were comfortably asleep in their arms; but it was to no avail.

The husbands were told that they had been deceived by the Devil and their own senses. They might have had the semblance of their wives in their beds, but actually they were far away at the Devil's dance beneath the oak. Hearing that from men in authority, the husbands were so confounded that they stood by while their wives were burned as witches. Oddly, it may never have occurred to them to ask why creditable people should have been snooping around a blasted oak at midnight hoping to see a witches' dance.

The quaint town of Verneuil, seventy miles west of Paris, site of a famous battle between the English and French in 1424, became briefly famous again in 1561, when five local witches were found guilty of changing themselves into cats and attending a sabbat, where they danced on the back of the Devil, who was present in the shape of a huge goat. They were burned, of course.

Three years later, a witch and three wizards suffered the same fate after confessing under torture that they had also worshipped the Devil in the form of a goat. But their crime was far worse, for they had prepared deadly ointments at his direction and had smeared them on sheep pens in order to kill the sheep. Unquestionably, many crimes were committed in which witchcraft served as a contributory factor; but those only spurred the witch hunters on in their quest for victims, whether guilty or innocent.

Exaggerated claims by witches often brought drastic results, as was the case of a master wizard named Trois Echelles, who was burned in Paris in 1571. Before his execution, he boasted that he had twelve hundred accomplices and that the total number of witches in France exceeded one hundred thousand. He revealed the names of his alleged confederates and thereby started a full-fledged witch hunt of his own.

Whether Trois Echelles was hoping to incriminate some of his enemies through false charges or was merely making a show of bravado so that he could go out in grand style, the net result was the same. His descriptions of sacrifices to the Devil, the debaucheries committed with youthful witches, the unguents that they prepared for the destruction of men and beasts, simply fanned the flames of fanatacism still higher.

One country that enjoyed immunity from the witch craze at this period was Sweden. There, although the power of witchcraft was recognized, it was evidently somewhat respected. In 1563, during the early stages of a seven-year war with Denmark, four witches were employed as secret weapons by King Eric XIV of

Sweden, who apparently wanted them to raise storms that would wreck the powerful Danish fleet. If so, the results were disappointing, for Denmark came out ahead in the long, though somewhat futile, struggle.

Eric himself became so deranged in 1567 that he could have been regarded as personally bewitched. He fancied that his brother John was reigning in his stead and when he temporarily recovered his reason the next year, he issued a proclamation ordering a general thanksgiving for his delivery from the attacks of the Devil, further evidence of his belief in witchcraft. Later, he relapsed and was soon deposed by his brother John.

By curious coincidence, when Eric became King of Sweden, due to the sudden death of his father in 1560, he was about to embark for England, hoping to marry Queen Elizabeth I. He never did, but they had a mutual belief in witchcraft. In 1563, while Eric was hiring his storm-makers, Elizabeth was issuing a statute against witchcraft in England, to open an era of persecution.

Politics vied with superstition in producing that edict. Elizabeth became Queen of England in 1558 and early in her reign, a wax image in her likeness was found with a pin thrust through its heart in Lincoln Inn's Field in London. In 1562, a plot was uncovered to kill Queen Elizabeth, so that Mary Stuart, Queen of Scots and next in succession to the English crown, could rule in her stead. Two of the conspirators were definitely charged with employing witchcraft toward their deadly purpose.

That helped trigger the witchcraft statute the next year; and an act against fantastic prophecies was included. That was partly because a prophetic poet of three centuries earlier, Thomas the Rhymer, had predicted that a French Queen would have a son who would rule all Britain. Some of the Rhymer's verses had been fulfilled; and it so happened that Mary Stuart had married King Francis II in 1558 and they had been crowned King and Queen of France a year later. When Francis died in 1560, Mary returned to Scotland and although she had no children, she was contemplating another marriage. So there was a chance she might have a son and become the "Queen of France" meant by the Rhymer's forecast.

Mary Stuart did marry again and she did have a son, who was proclaimed King of Scotland when she was forced to abdicate in 1567. When Queen Elizabeth died in 1603, he became King of England as well, and the prophecy of Thomas the Rhymer was fulfilled. By then, it was no longer Elizabeth's concern, but she had experienced plenty of scares during the intervening years. Plots against her life had been frequent, often with witchcraft involved to some degree.

One notable instance was the discovery, in 1578, of three wax images representing the queen and two of her courtiers; these bore mystic symbols and were stuck with sharp bristles. In 1580, a man was arrested for merely making a wax image of Elizabeth; and another case cropped up in 1589. In 1587, Mary Stuart was executed on trumped up charges of plotting against Elizabeth's life; and when Ferdinando Stanley, son of one of the judges, died suddenly in 1594, witchcraft again was suspect of rearing its ugly head.

Ferdinando was the fifth Earl of Derby and he suffered from a week of violent stomach ailments which no physicians could correctly diagnose until they found a wax image, hidden in the bedroom, with hair resembling the earl's twisted within the figure. Such evidence of witchcraft merely served to increase its potency, for the earl's condition became worse after he saw the image and within a few days after it was burned, in hope of destroying the witch, the earl died.

In the light of later opinion, the image could have been purposely planted to draw attention from a poison plot against the earl; if that was the case, it was doubly efficacious in that it played upon the victim's mind as well as his body. Such was the grip that belief in witchcraft held upon the public of that day; and the higher the rank, the greater the fear. Hence it was only logical that the queen, as prime target of all plotters, would encourage any law that discouraged witchcraft.

Unfortunately, the repercussions among the lowly were greater than in court circles. That wasn't too hard to understand, considering that any commoner accused of witchcraft would automatically gain a distinction that until then had been reserved almost exclusively for the nobility. That was proven in 1556, just three years after promulgation of the witchcraft statute, when Elizabeth Francis was brought to trial in an Essex town, on rather vague charges of bewitching a neighbor's infant son. Apparently, the woman thought she was a witch, or wanted to be a witch. Either way, it was enough for people to suspect that she really was a witch. So she revelled in the distinction and came up with a story that was to make history, and also make a lot of misery for a lot of people, herself included.

In her poor, pitiful, but forthright way, Elizabeth Francis became the prototype of a modern LSD inspired dropout, mugging a TV camera in defiance of the existing Establishment. The difference was that in her day, it was the Elizabethan Establishment, for the coincidence of the name "Elizabeth" must have occurred to the superstitious judges and to her superstitious self as well, to say nothing of super-superstitious Queen Elizabeth I.

Eliminating such technicalities, Elizabeth Francis really went to town. The big reason she was considered to be a witch, outside of the way she mumbled, cursed, or cast a mean eye, as about everybody else in Essex was doing in those days, was this: Her grandmother had been a witch.

Good thinking, that. It was a known fact that witches breed witches, though nobody had really admitted it, because until then, witches had been a subject of whispers, not talk. So that left it for Mrs. Francis to prove, which she did, before the judges of her day. She did it just as happily as if she were extolling the Chicago Seven before the Supreme Court of the United States. What was more, she sold it.

She claimed that her dear old grandmother had initiated her into the sorority of witchery when she was only twelve years old by giving her a white-spotted cat named Sathan. She didn't specify whether the cat was black with white spots, or white with black spots; nor did she emphasize that the name "Sathan" might have been interpreted as "Satan." She left that for the judges to decide and, as customary in such cases, they decided against her.

However, once Mrs. Francis had established Sathan as an entity, there was no stopping her. Sathan, it turned out, was a talking cat, who asked her, in a deep hollow tone, just what she wanted; and when she told him, Sathan went out and got it for her, just like that.

Sathan brought her a flock of sheep, some white, some black, possibly to match his own markings. What happened to them, she didn't know, because by then she was more interested in the prospective husband that the clever cat produced for her. After he abused her, but then refused to marry her, she complained to Sathan, who touched the reluctant lover with his paw and caused him to wither away and die. Thinking that she might have a child as a result of this brief union, she again asked Sathan's advice and the fantastic feline recommended a special preparation which she concocted, drank, and put a prompt end to her problem.

Sathan next beguiled Christopher Francis into marrying her, but either would not, or could not, guarantee them domestic tranquility. Six months after the birth of a daughter, Mrs. Francis tired of her husband's cursing and the baby's howling, so she appealed to Sathan for further aid. The cat obliged by causing the child to die, but when that failed to bring quiet to the household, Mrs. Francis urged Sathan to take direct action against her obstreperous husband.

Obligingly, the cat transformed itself into a toad and squatted in one of Christopher's shoes. When the man touched the squirmy thing with his toe, he was so shocked that he went suddenly lame and remained so for a dozen years, up to the time of his wife's trial for witchcraft. Meanwhile, Elizabeth Francis had decided to dispose of Sathan, one good reason being that the cat, in order to fulfill a wish, invariably demanded that she prick herself with a pin, so that she could feed it a goodly supply of her blood along with its regular diet of bread and milk.

Mrs. Francis showed the judges pin marks that she had carried on her body from years back and told how one day she had swapped the cat for a cake cooked by an older woman called Mother Waterhouse, who was intrigued by Sathan's wish-granting powers. Mother Waterhouse was also charged with witchcraft and gladly told the judges how she often assigned tasks to the talented tabby; and she, too, showed pin marks to prove it.

Mother Waterhouse had enjoined her familiar to kill three pigs belonging to a troublesome neighbor; and after that, three geese owned by a neighbor she disliked even more. When a brewery made too much noise at night, Sathan soured its product so that Mother Waterhouse could sleep. He afflicted one mean neighbor with a lingering malady from which he died, so Mother Waterhouse had Sathan do the same with her own husband, of whom she had tired.

Mrs. Francis had kept Sathan in a basket, but Mother Waterhouse, finding that inconvenient, had managed to have him switch permanently from his form of a cat into that of a toad, so he could live in a pot instead. But her daughter, Joan, who was eighteen, admitted calling upon Sathan to annoy a twelve-year-old girl named Agnes Brown and he had assumed the shape of a huge black dog in order to accomplish that mission.

Joan Waterhouse, too, was charged with witchcraft and little Agnes Brown, who had been either lamed or partly paralyzed by her frightening experience, was called upon as a key witness. Not to be outdone, she added still more fanciful details, giving the shaggy dog a face like an ape's, a pair of horns like a devil's and a silver whistle which he carried on a chain around his neck. The young girl quoted dialogues between herself and the weird creature, in which she countered all his fiendish threats with pious responses, until he admitted that he belonged to Mother Waterhouse. That satisfied the court.

Under the terms of the Elizabethan Act, anyone causing death through witchcraft was to suffer the death penalty as punishment, so Mother Waterhouse, by her own admissions, was declared guilty of that charge and hanged a few days later. Her daughter Joan, who had only tried her hand once, and even then might have been ignorant of what would result, was acquitted. Mrs.

Francis was convicted on the lesser charge of having used witchcraft to do harm, which carried the comparatively mild penalty of a year's imprisonment for a first offender. Possibly her admissions of causing death were doubted; or the fact that such deaths dated back before the passage of the act may have worked in her favor.

Anyway, her luck didn't hold. A few years later, she again meddled in harmful witchcraft and received another year's sentence, though the edict allowed the death penalty for a second offender. After a few more years, she had another try, was caught and summarily hanged as a third offender.

This case is deserving of detailed mention as it set an insidious pattern for the witch mania that followed. Superficially, it seemed fair and liberal; but there can be no fairness or liberality where prejudice and superstition are involved. Throughout the European continent, standardized questions, based on inquisitorial concepts, had given most witch hunts a stereotyped status. Apparently, English lawmakers thought that by letting the alleged witches speak for themselves, an impartial verdict could be reached. Yet often they condemned themselves voluntarily by echoing the stupid beliefs in which they, like their accusers, were so deeply steeped.

That happened even though physical tortures were banned in England and mental panic was lessened because the death penalty was hanging, not burning. Alleged pacts with the Devil were uncommon among English witches of the period; rather, they were suspected of harboring familiars, or imps, not just as cats, toads or dogs, but in the shape of lambs, rabbits, skunks and even spiders or flies, as well as imaginary monsters. These were suckled on witch's blood, so any peculiar marks or blemishes on a witch's body were evident of such.

This put all the more burden of proof on persons accused of witchcraft and when children became prime witnesses in trials and let their imaginations run riot, almost anything could happen. In many instances, both accusations and evidence were so preposterous and self-contradictory, even in that unenlightened era, that acquittals resulted; but far from being a good sign, that in itself was a highly deceptive factor. Enough new angles were being steadily admitted to increase the number of accusations and rouse the public to a greater fervor against witchcraft in general.

At a mass trial of Essex witches in 1582, one woman was accused by her stepdaughter, age eight, of keeping two toads as familiars, one black, the other white, named Tom and Robin respectively. Not to be outdone, another girl of seven told the judges that her mother kept six blackbirds as familiars, with six more in reserve. As many as eighteen persons were accused in this all-out witch hunt; and some were executed, though estimates vary as to the exact number.

At a third such trial in 1589, an eleven-year-old boy and his younger brother supplied the evidence needed to hang their old grandmother; two others were convicted on equally flimsy evidence. All three were executed in less than two hours after they were sentenced, establishing some sort of a record; and all three were named Joan. That may have set a precedent, because a modern commentator on witchcraft has pointed out that over the years the mortality rates on Joans has been far higher than that of any other name.

All this and more will be summarized later. But at present, we are still concerned with the rise of the witchcraft craze in England, which so far had hardly hit its stride.

8
Skeptics Versus Believers

It is difficult to estimate the number of witch trials held in England during the forty years following the Elizabethan Act instituted in 1453, but some calculations run as high as two thousand. This is based on the assumption that the two hundred cases officially recorded represented only about ten percent of the grand total, as English trials were not only regional, but local, conducted under almost any auspices.

This contrasted with the more uniform procedures in the European countries where witch trials were flourishing in their well-established fashion. However, English witch hunters were prompt to borrow anything that was helpful. Many went by the rules laid down in *Malleus Maleficarum* and those of later authors who insisted that witches be harshly judged. Among these was Jean Bodin, a French monk who later became a professor of law and whose most famous work, *Demonomania of Witches*, appeared in 1480, and eventually became a classic in the field. Bodin visited England a year later and his book was well received there because of its scholarly style; hence it did much to speed the continuing campaign against witchcraft.

The result was a surprising counter-attack by an English writer named Reginald Scot, who was also disturbed by the mass trial of falsely accused witches that took place in 1482. Scot's book, *The Discovery of Witchcraft*, appeared two years later and proved to be a veritable thunderbolt of common sense. In a matter of some 250 chapters, Scot questioned the sources cited by Bodin and others, belittling many things attributed to witchcraft as the "old wives' tales" that they most probably were.

This sample from Scot's opening blast shows the skeptical style of the entire volume, in which he heaped well-chosen ridicule upon witchmongers, as he termed them:

> *The fables of witchcraft have taken so fast hold and deep root in the heart of man that few or none can nowadays with patience endure the hand and correction of God. For if any adversity, grief, sickness, loss of children, corn, cattle, or liberty happen unto them, by and by, they exclaim upon witches. . . .*
>
> *Such faithless people are also persuaded that neither hail nor snow, thunder nor lightning, rain nor tempestuous winds come from the heavens at the commandment of God; but are raised by the cunning and power of witches and conjurors; insomuch as a clap of thunder or a gale of wind is no sooner heard, but either they run*

to ring bells, or cry out to burn witches; or else burn consecrated things, hoping by the smoke thereof, to drive the Devil out of the air, as though spirits could be frightened away with such external toys....

Scot's reference to bells was highly appropriate, for it was solemnly supposed that the sure way to ground a witch flying to the sabbat was by ringing church bells. By that token, witches should have been dropping all over town on certain nights. The fact that they weren't was easy to explain: When a witch saw a church-bell swinging, she flew faster than the sound in order to escape it. Evidently witches had jet-propelled broomsticks, even away back then; otherwise, they couldn't have broken the sound barrier. Anyway, at least the church bells scared them.

Scot cited a case of alleged witchcraft that he personally investigated. His account is interesting indeed, representing a welcome relief from the small-minded gullibility then so prevalent:

At the assizes held at Rochester in 1581, one Margaret Simons was arraigned for witchcraft at the instigation of foolish and malicious persons and specially by the means of one John Ferrall, vicar of that parish, with whom I talked about the matter and found him both foolishly infatuated in the cause, and enviously bent toward her; and, which is worse, as unable to make a good account of himself as she whom he accused. That which he, for his part, laid to the poor woman's charge was this:

His son, being an ungracious boy and an apprentice to a clothier, passed one day by her house; when by chance, her little dog barked at him. Which thing, the boy taking in evil part, drew his knife and pursued him therewith even to her door; whom she rebuked with some such words as the boy disdained and yet nevertheless would not be persuaded to depart in a long time.

At last he returned to his master's house and within five or six days fell sick. Then was called to mind the fray betwixt the dog and the boy: insomuch as the vicar (who thought himself so privileged, as he little mistrusted that God would visit his children with sickness) did so calculate; as he found, partly through his own judgment and partly (as he himself told me) by the relation of other witches, that his son was by her bewitched. He also told me that his son (being as

> it were, past all cure) received perfect health at the hands of another witch.
>
> He proceeded yet further against her, affirming that always in his parish church, when he desired to read most plainly, his voice so failed him, as he could scant be heard at all. Which he could impute, he said, to nothing else but to her enchantment. When I advertised the poor woman hereof, as being desirous to hear what she could say for herself, she told me that in very deed his voice did much fail him, specially when he strained himself to speak loudest. Howbeit, she said that at all times his voice was hoarse and low; which thing I perceived to be true. . . .

Working from that, Scot checked with reputable people of the parish and not only found them in accord, but learned that the vicar had earlier been afflicted with a lung ailment that accounted for his hoarseness. Evidently unwilling to admit that his voice was failing, he had imagined witchcraft to be responsible. This was evidently brought up in court by Scot, for poor Margaret Simons was acquitted; but Scot, still the complete skeptic, added this significant comment at the end of the account:

> And truly, if one of the jury had not been wiser than the others, she would have been condemned thereupon; and upon other as ridiculous matters as this. For the name of a witch is so odious, and her power so feared among the common people, that if the honestest body living should chance to be arraigned thereupon, she shall hardly escape condemnation.

Scot's book is filled with literary jabs at the stupid superstitions of his age, but where he dealt the real convincers was in special chapters where he compared the alleged, but unproven marvels attributed to witches with the pretended feats of wizardry performed by mountebanks and jugglers then appearing at fairs in London and other parts of England. He explained how a conjuror could apparently stab himself with a knife, yet suffer no injury, by using a trick knife with a retractable blade that slid back into the handle. He also described knives with fake blades that could apparently be thrust through the performer's arm, which he termed "a pitiful sight, without hurt or injury."

Another knife, with a semicircular cut-out in the center of the blade, was used "to cut half your nose asunder and to heal it again presently, without any salve." From there, Scot went on to bigger and better marvels, the most spectacular was "to cut off a man's head and to lay it on a platter, which the jugglers call the decollation of John Baptist."

If Scot's book had gained the circulation it deserved, it might have spelled an early end to witch hunts, and indeed to witchcraft, so far as belief in witchcraft can ever be dispelled. Both skeptical and satirical, Scot subjected all serious, sanctimonious supporters of the supposedly supernatural to a ridicule that should have squelched them; and perhaps did, temporarily. But he ran head-on into an insurmountable obstacle that nullified the book's potential good.

In 1589, a marriage was arranged between King James of Scotland and Princess Anne of Denmark, whose ship encountered heavy winds and was forced to take shelter in a Norwegian harbor, where it remained stormbound. So James braved the North Sea to claim his bride and they spent some months in Copenhagen before starting for Scotland, only to encounter a still more furious tempest that almost wrecked the royal bark before it reached Leith, on May 1, 1590.

All Scotland talked of the king's miraculous deliverance until witchcraft took the limelight in a town outside of Edinburgh. There, a young and personable serving girl named Gellie Duncan displayed such ability at healing people's ailments that her employer, David Seaton, decided that the Devil had a hand in it. His suspicions were increased because Gellie had a sneaky way of going out nights, which in the light of later developments, could have been quite justified, if only because Gellie wanted to sneak away from Seaton.

Whatever the case, Seaton exerted his authority as a Deputy Bailiff to put Gellie to the torture. Details as to the torture differ, but all were reasonably gruesome. However, the final test was to find a witch's mark on Gellie, which they did, after much frustration. It was found on her throat, which gives an idea as to how frustrated they were until they found it. When they found it, Gellie talked, not just because her tongue was loosened, but also her throat; probably from things like ropes.

Gellie admitted that she had sold her soul to the Devil, but that she had not done it alone. She had worked at the instigation of higher-uppers, whom she named, some forty in all, mostly of a respectable and influential sort. An older woman, Agnes Sampson, wilted under an hour's torture and began talking as fancifully as Gellie had. Both accused a schoolteacher named Cunningham of secretly practicing witchcraft under the name of Dr. John Fian and lining up an assortment of more than two hundred witches, with a sprinkling of warlocks, to do the Devil's bidding. On special occasions, they went to the shore and embarked in large sieves, called riddles, to a haunted church farther up the coast. There Dr. Fian blew upon candles, which instantly lighted, revealing the Devil himself, occupying the old pulpit.

His Satanic Majesty had a terrible face with great, burning eyes, a nose like an eagle's beak, a body like iron and claws for hands and feet. He wore a black cap and gown; and his voice was gruff indeed, as he called the roll of his followers and demanded their homage, which they duly gave. After delivering a vitriolic preachment on the virtues of evil, the Devil had them dig up a newly buried corpse on which they feasted, while imbibing great quantities of fine wine that Satan personally supplied.

Following that, Gellie Duncan provided music and the Devil led off a dance with a sprightly witch named Euphemia Macalzean, the daughter of a Scottish lord, and the rest cavorted merrily until dawn under the watchful eye of a crazy old warlock named Gray Meill, who acted as the Devil's doorkeeper. But malice lay beneath this merriment. These meetings began prior to the marriage of King James and Princess Anne; and the chief reason for each witches' sabbat was to discuss ways and means of preventing that event.

The storm that first delayed Princess Anne was evidently brewed by Danish witches and Satan counted on Scottish sorcery to dispose of King James permanently. The Devil himself furnished a further delaying action by creating a heavy fog that prevented the king's ship from sailing; but the mighty tempest that almost doomed James and his bride was the result of coordinated effort by the entire witch clan. On an appointed night, they cruised about in their bewitched waterproof sieves until they met the Devil, who performed a ritual of throwing a cat into the sea, which immediately raised huge waves. Satan himself put out to sea amid the storm he had created, looming larger and larger like a giant haystack until he disappeared beyond the billowy horizon. The witches, having done their duty, managed to outrace the storm to shore, where they gloatingly took refuge in the haunted church to await the Devil's return.

When King James heard of these confessions, he took a personal interest in the trials and interrogated the key witches himself. When they blamed the Devil for inciting them and quoted him as saying that King James was the greatest enemy he ever had and that there would be no peace on earth for demons until they got rid of such a scourge, the king was highly flattered. As a firm believer in his own divine right to rule, he felt that he had scored a personal triumph by riding out a storm that the Devil himself had raised. But if the accused witches were seeking to save their own hides by their wild fabrications, they overdid it by injecting too much truth.

Agnes Sampson, for one, admitted that she had prepared a hellish potion or powder, hoping to apply it to some garment belonging to the king and thus bewitch him to death. To prove her ability at witchcraft, she told King James the exact words that he had spoken to Princess Anne on their wedding night in Norway. That, to the highly impressionistic young monarch, apparently proved that all the other statements must be true; for when one accused woman was acquitted, King James not only commanded that she be retried and convicted; he also threatened to have the jurors tried for being parties to witchcraft. So they reconsidered their verdict and threw themselves upon the king's mercy, which was granted.

In all, some thirty persons were condemned and executed at

these trials and they all tallied in their descriptions of the witch's sabbat in the haunted church. That raised the very plausible possibility that the entire group was duped and dominated by a master plotter who masqueraded as the Devil at the unholy meetings, and hoped to use some of his deluded human tools — most notably Agnes Sampson — to poison or otherwise physically injure the king under the pretended guise of witchery.

Candidate for such a mastermind was the Earl of Bothwell, whose uncle, the previous Earl, had married Mary Queen of Scots after the murder of her husband, Darnley, the father of King James. To have put over such an imposture on the whole wretched crew, Bothwell would have needed a skilled accomplice to hand pick and manage the members of the ever-increasing coven, while Bothwell himself kept tabs of what was happening at court.

Dr. John Fian could readily have served as such a go-between, because it was he who invoked the Devil and managed all the theatricals at the haunted church. Furthermore, he alone of all the accused persons refused utterly to confess anything, even though subjected to tortures far more hideous than any imaginary devil rites. They squeezed everything possible out of him, except words; he knew that if he told them what they wanted to hear, they would still continue to torture him in order to expand their new line of interrogation. Instead, he thwarted his torturers by bearing the ordeals until they rendered him insensible and unable to talk.

Thus Dr. John Fian went to his death and the full truth of Scotland's most famous case of witchcraft was never known. Whatever else lay behind it, King James still believed that the greatest and most dangerous threat was witchcraft, so he took it at face value. A man of some literary ability, he proceeded to write a book, *Demonology*, which treated the subject very seriously, and helped usher in a new era in which superstition reigned.

9
The Witch Finders and Their Ways

In his famous *Demonology*, which first appeared in 1597, King James of Scotland proclaimed:

> *The fearful abounding at this time and in this country of those detestable slaves of the Devil, the witches and enchanters, hath moved me, beloved reader, to despatch in post, this following treatise of mine, not in any wise to serve as a show of my own learning and ingenuity, but only to resolve the doubting hearts of many, both that such assaults of Satan are most certainly practiced and that the instrument thereof merits most severely to be punished.* ...
>
> *Witches ought to be put to death, according to the law of God, the civil and imperial law and the municipal law of all Christian nations; yea, to spare the life and not strike when God bids strike and so severely punish in so odious a treason against God, is not only unlawful, but doubtless as great a sin in the magistrate as was Saul's sparing Agag.* ...

That made it open season on witches throughout all Scotland. But James had his eye on far greater territory and he achieved his aim in 1603, when he became King of England as well. Though he could not order witches burned in England, James did the next best thing. He ordered all available copies of Scot's *Discovery of Witchcraft* to be seized and burned, at the same time arranging for new editions of his own *Demonology* to be printed, so that the public would be limited to a one-sided and thoroughly prejudiced view of the subject. James also induced parliament to supplant the old Elizabethan Act against witchcraft with a new statute, passed in 1604, making it a capital offense to attempt to injure anyone by witchcraft, regardless of whether it succeeded; and a pact with the Devil came under that general head.

Opinions varied as to the effect of the edict. Some felt that King James injected new life into a dying superstition; for although there was a decline in death sentences during his reign, they might have dropped off faster. Others, however, attributed the decline to the severity of the statute itself, proving that it discouraged witchcraft more strongly than before and thereby accomplished its main aim. In any case, the high mark of his regime was reached in 1612, when a feud broke out between two ancient witches, Mother Demdike and Mother Chattox, each of whom had taught their craft to various members of their families, who in turn operated as a combined coven which held sabbats at a place called Malking Tower in the Pendle Forest of Lancashire. Each apparently began blaming acts of witchcraft on the others, with the result that both old crones and a few of their offspring were put in jail to await trial.

That brought about a reconciliation among the rest, who held a sabbat at the tower to plan the rescue of the prisoners, by demolishing the local jail. Whether they planned to do it by witchcraft or gunpowder was never proven, because the law gained wind of it before they got around to it. Practically the whole coven was arrested on charges and countercharges of varying degrees of witchcraft. From the complex welter sprang a surprise witness, Jennet Device, age nine, whose mother, Elizabeth Device, was the daughter of Old Mother Demdike.

Too young to have been taken into the coven, but old enough to be allowed to stand around and listen, Jennet came through with enough juicy reports to undermine the whole Demdike-Chattox setup better than they could have done with the Lancashire jail. Little Jennet told how a familiar called "Ball" had appeared as a brown dog to help her mother kill people, whose names she presumably gave. Her evidence was supported by her brother James, who was in his twenties, and apparently the retarded member of the family.

James believed in about anything, for he had not only seen the dog named Ball, he had watched his mother make clay images that Jennet mentioned; and he talked about a mysterious hare that accosted him on his way home from church, but vanished on command. The judges checked that back with Jennet, who, rather than be outdone, told them that James had a dog of his own named "Dandy" who helped him bewitch people to death, so James, just for trying to be too smart, wound up in the bullpen with the rest of the suspects.

The net result: Out of about twenty prisoners put on trial, ten were hanged. Mother Demdike escaped by dying in jail, but Elizabeth Device went the rope route, along with her stupid son James and her eleven-year-old daughter Alison, who must have been a little dumber or not quite as smart as her nine-year-old sister Jennet, who had turned state's evidence and was accordingly exonerated.

From then on, smart children spoke their piece at witchcraft trials and King James, to his credit, began to doubt them along with his own opinions until he died in 1625, leaving the field wide open for further frauds. Among those was another case in the Pendle Forest, which occured in 1633, and was triggered by a boy named Edmund Robertson, whose father was a woodcutter. Possibly young Edmund had heard tales of earlier witchery; in any case, he decided that an old woman called Mother Dickenson rated as a witch.

So Edmund told the local magistrates that while roaming through the woods, he met two greyhounds, which he tried to excite into chasing a rabbit; but both refused to stir. So he struck one with a switch and it promptly turned itself into the form of Mother Dickenson, while the other became a little boy whom Edmund did not recognize. Mother Dickenson offered Edmund money if he would sell his soul to the Devil, but he stoutly refused, so she took a bridle from her pocket and shook it above the little boy who had been a greyhound and turned him into a horse.

Mother Dickenson then snatched up Edmund, sprang upon the horse and galloped with the speed of wind through forests, fields, bogs and rivers, to a large barn, where Edmund saw seven old women pulling at seven halters and bringing down meat, butter, bread, milk and puddings on which they feasted, along with other witches who crowded into the barn — as many as sixty in all. During the festivities, the boy managed to slip out unnoticed and run home.

Young Edmund was taken from church to church, so he could point out women whom he had seen at the sabbat. He identified some thirty in all, and among them was none other than Jennet Device, who as a little girl, had called the turn on the Malking Tower coven some twenty-two years before. Seventeen were condemned, but escaped the hangman when a local bishop persuaded King Charles I to conduct a fuller investigation of the flimsy case. Edmund's story was exploded and it was generally conceded that the boy's father had encouraged him in the hoax. The elder Robinson had planned to collect blackmail money from well-to-do women by telling them that Edmund would point them out if they didn't pay.

In short, this case and others show that witchcraft was developing into a lucrative racket, which reached its peak in 1645, when Oliver Cromwell and his Puritan forces gained their decisive victory over the Royalists in England's Civil War. An opportunist named Matthew Hopkins, recognizing that a new regime was due, appointed himself Witch Finder General and set out through Essex and adjacent counties with a retinue of assistants skilled in the art of recognizing and rounding up witches. Each town was charged a varying fee, plus expenses, for such services; and for each executed witch, Hopkins and his helpers received a bonus of twenty shillings.

Hopkins knew all the accepted methods of proving suspects to be witches, such as demanding them to recite the Lord's Prayer without stumbling over a syllable; or by weighing the accused against the church bible. But he favored a system specially recommended by King James in his *Demonology* — that of "swimming" a witch, by tossing her into a pool of water. If she floated, she was guilty and was duly executed; if she sank, she was innocent, but was apt to drown in the process, which was good riddance in itself.

Looking for witch marks was an old established test that by this time had been greatly improved by shaving a suspect's entire body, so the slightest mark could be detected, even one hidden beneath an eyebrow. The harder to find, the more likely the mark was of the Devil's making. To clinch it, however, Hopkins and his crew specialized in witch-pricking — jabbing witch marks with pins or pointed implements on the theory that if they didn't hurt or bleed, witchery must be responsible.

Since some moles or warts were immune to this, the witch prickers frequently proved their point; but if frustrated, they began jabbing less sensitive parts of the suspect's body, hoping to find invisible marks, which were truly the Devil's work. Here, it is highly probable that Hopkins and others of his ilk had been reading Scot's *Discovery of Witchcraft*, which by then was back in circulation, and that they were using the trick knives with blades that slid into the handle, so they could apparently jab witches deeply, yet draw no blood.

The Witch Finder General also kept suspects bound without food or water for twenty-four hours at a time, not just to break down their morale, but so that constant watch could be kept to see if any of their imps tried to contact them. Any insect, a wasp, a fly or a moth, could be one of the witch's familiars in disguise; and if the watchers were unable to kill it before it flew away, its fiendish intent was established. Since the watchers were usually members of the Witch Finder's crew, they naturally didn't try; not with twenty shillings riding on the outcome.

Estimates as to the total number of alleged witches executed through the machinations of Matthew Hopkins and his witch finders run from two hundred upward — all within a single year. By dint of his self-established authority, Hopkins could have kept the figures to himself; and wisely. Despite that, the extent of his operations was so appalling that it roused public indignation. And when Hopkins was openly denounced by a clergyman named John Gaul, the Witch Finder General decided to discard his fake title and retire to the hinterlands with his loot.

Within another year, Matthew Hopkins was dead. According to one account, a mob caught up with him and decided that he should take a witch test for himself. So they bound him hand and foot and swam him; but he didn't come up. The story, however, has been doubted, another version being that he died "peaceably" after a long sickness of a consumption. Here, the word "peaceably" is highly questionable. One of the most strongly accepted notions regarding witches was their ability to make their enemies waste away; and anyone who thought he was a victim of such a process was apt to aid and abet it through his own belief.

So Matthew Hopkins, Witch Finder General, may have worried himself into a mysterious malady of his own making, unless the smarter witches who had eluded his devices got together in a secret coven and put a bona fide spell upon him.

Prosecutions for witchcraft persisted during the Puritan period under Oliver Crowell as Lord Protector, but the opposing Royalists were quite as steeped in superstition. They actually believed that Cromwell had personally made a pact with the Devil; otherwise, his dull stupid army of Roundheads could never have defeated their dashing Cavaliers. One harsh critic branded Cromwell as "a brave, bad man, with all the wickedness against which damnation is pronounced and for which hell fire is prepared." So when London was swept by a terrible tempest on September 3, 1658, the day when Cromwell died, his adversaries insisted that it was bringing the Devil to carry away his arch-disciple, as if he really deserved such consideration.

But after King Charles II ascended to the throne in 1660, executions for witchcraft became more scattered under the Restoration; and during the next half century, with the rise of more liberal judges and the improvement of court procedures, trials for witchcraft dwindled. The last hanging in England occured in 1684, though one took place in Scotland as late as 1722.

Oddly, the greatest flare-up in this period of marked decline took place in staid New England, in 1692, where a group of teen-aged girls, inspired by the voodoo tales of a West Indian woman named Tituba, began meeting at a parsonage in Salem, Massachusetts. There, they went into convulsive fits that a local physician diagnosed as bewitchment. When asked who tormented them, the teen-agers named three of the most eccentric beldames in the area and added Tituba for good measure. To save themselves, the scared suspects began naming others, while the youthful accusers continued to throw fits and blame still more people for them.

Soon, all Salem was in the act. People not only said they had seen witches flying to sabbats on broomsticks; they told how they had been carried along with them. They described weird lights, grotesque demons, and feats of strength performed by accused persons that could only have been done through diabolical aid. For example, one man was accused of having thrust his forefinger into the muzzle of a gun and lifting it just that easily. Considering the ponderous muskets of those days, that was not just superhuman, it was supernatural. Others blamed witches for pigs that vanished; oxen that stampeded and swam rivers; cattle that danced, talked and finally dropped dead; along with other phenomena.

They only wished that witches would dance and drop dead, which nineteen out of the 150 accused obligingly did, each at the end of a rope, before this travesty of justice completed its brief run of idiotic delight in 1693.

By the 1700's, however, all this was on its way out, not only in England, but throughout Europe and even in America. Yet there is still one rift amid the clouds of gloom. It cannot be said that all these witches died in vain. For witchcraft still lives — and how!

10
Vampires: Devils in Human Form

Belief in vampires, those bloodthirsty entities that prowl by night in human form, is so maliciously and malignantly related to witchcraft, that to a marked degree they may be classed as interchangeable. As a prime case in point, one good way to become a vampire is to start out as a witch or warlock and stay with it, with death representing a very trifling transition from the one status to the other.

There are, of course, other and perhaps worse ways of becoming a vampire; and the subject has so many facets that it unquestionably exceeds the bounds of witchcraft and becomes a part of ghostlore. However, witches have ghostly privileges on occasion, so there, again, the twain meet, or at least cross orbits. But a vampire, in the most popularly accepted sense, belongs to ghostdom because it represents the spirit of a dead person who has returned to the realm of the living. However, unlike a ghost, which is a mere phantom that assumes human semblance, the vampire has the same body that it had in life. Hence, vampires are neither dead nor alive, but living in death, so they have accordingly been termed the "Undead," and as such, their functions can be horrendous indeed. Yet with all the lore that has come to light on vampires, it was not until 1733 that John Henry Zopfius, a renowned German scholar, summarized their case as follows:

> *Vampires come out of their graves at night time, rush upon people sleeping in their beds, suck out all their blood and destroy them. They attack men, women and children, sparing neither age nor sex. Those who come under their malign influence complain of suffocation and a great loss of spirits; soon afterward, they expire. Some of them, being asked at the point of death what is the matter with them, give reply that they suffer in the manner related from people lately dead. . . .*
>
> *Upon which, the bodies of those people, being dug out of their graves, appear in all parts, as the nostrils, cheeks, breast and mouth to be turgid and full of blood. Their countenances are fresh and ruddy; their nails and hair, very much grown. Though they have been much longer dead than many other bodies which are completely putrefied, not the least sign of corruption is visible upon them. Those persons who are destroyed by them, also become vampires after their death; hence to prevent such an evil from spreading, it becomes necessary to drive a stake through the dead body, from whence on such occasion, the blood flows as if the person were still alive. Sometimes the body is dug out of the grave and burned to ashes, whereupon, all disturbances cease.*

The description as given by Zopfius was based on his study of vampirism in Hungary and Serbia from the Middle Ages; but it goes farther back. The vampire legend can be traced from ancient Babylonia and Assyria to the later days of imperial Rome, with their stories of the so-called demons, or Lamias, who took human form and thrived on either the blood or the vigor of their chosen victims. Hecate, the Roman goddess so closely associated with witchcraft, was identified with vampirism as well, forming another link between the two. When such pagan beliefs carried over to the Christian Era, it was simpler to blame them on the Devil, rather than charge them off to mere superstition. That was notably true in the Roman province of Dacia, which occupied the area of modern Rumania and the adjacent mountain region of Transylvania.

There, the natives already believed that death was merely a transition from one state of existence to another, so they found the vampire concept quite acceptable. In the centuries that followed, Dacia became a crossroad of barbarian invasions that overran the Roman Empire, but a stalwart portion of the populace managed to retain their individuality along with Roman culture and civilization.

This was accomplished in part by the setting up of feudal systems, particularly in the more rugged regions, under the leadership of chieftains known as *voivodes*, who were recognized as rulers, governors, or officials of lesser degree, according to the time and circumstance. Though they paid tribute to Hungary and were nominally under that nation's control, many of the voivodes enjoyed special privileges, which were the equivalent of independence.

However, after the fall of Constantinople in 1453, the victorious Turks moved northward and began appointing voivodes of their own choice. One of these was Vlad IV, son of a very ferocious voivode, whose example he decided to surpass. Having won the confidence of the Turks, he began slaughtering persons who opposed him by driving stakes through their bodies and feasting among his victims. As a result, he became known as *Dracul*, a word meaning devil, and he also won himself the title of Vlad the Impaler.

Even the Turkish sultan was so shocked by this that he sent an emissary to order Vlad to desist. True to his Dracul reputation, Vlad impaled the envoy along with a new crop of victims. That brought the sultan with such a huge army that Vlad cleared out before he arrived, leaving behind a veritable forest of staked out bodies of men, women and children. A new voivode, Radu, was appointed and held office for a dozen years; but following that, Vlad the Impaler once again became voivode of the Walachian province where he had committed his merciless crimes.

This made an odd preamble to the theory of vampirism that was to develop so strongly during the following centuries. The obvious question, of course, is just why Vlad, alias Dracul, a living monster, should have driven stakes through living forms of ordinary mortals, when that treatment was usually reserved for the dead bodies of suspected vampires? A grimly plausible answer might be that Vlad himself was actually a vampire and, as a member of the Undead, delighted in doing to the living what they should have done to him.

Nearly three hundred years elapsed between the time of Vlad the Impaler and John Henry Zopfius, whose scholarly comments on vampires have already been noted. Throughout that period, legends, lore and rumors were tempered with observable facts to shape apparently solid theories regarding vampires. Unlike the early proponents of witchcraft, who were ready not only to credit any wild claims but outmatch them with wilder notions of their own, students of the vampire situation were skeptical in their approach and guarded in their opinions. This probably averted appalling consequences of the sort brought on by the authors of *Malleus Maleficarum* and other maudlin literary outbursts.

A decade after Zopfius had summed the vampire situation as he saw it, Dom Augustin Calmet, a French author, took a decidedly more conservative stand. Confronted by a deluge of data concerning a completely new type of ghost or specter — the vampire — reported from Hungary and adjacent lands, Dom Calmet asked this question: How could a corpse, encased in a coffin beneath five feet of earth, return to the upper air and cause all the remarkable effects attributed to it?

And if that were not enough, how could it return to the same grave and be found fresh and full of blood, exactly like a living body? Could such corpses penetrate the earth without disturbing it, just as water filters through the soil, or vapors arise from the ground? If so, since their bodies were spectral, how could they suck the blood of human beings? Finally, assuming that all these phenomena were actual, Dom Calmet felt that he and all other investigators of the subject would be snagged in a total dilemma if they even asked whether such apparitions were purely natural or utterly miraculous.

With the passing years, hundreds of new reports offered answers that were even more fantastic than the questions themselves, leaving the final verdict more baffling than ever. In 1897, an author named Bram Stoker penned a weird novel entitled *Dracula*, featuring a monstrous villain who was undoubtedly patterned after the real life Dracul of four centuries before. The important point was that though Stoker's story was fictional, it gave an accurate summation of the supposed facts pertaining to vampires up to that date, all fully acceptable to persons believing in the existence of such entities; for example: Vampires can live indefinitely, becoming younger with time, provided they obtain the proper blood diet, on which alone they feast, partaking of no other food. Vampires cast no shadows, nor can their reflections be seen in mirrors. They have tremendous physical strength and can transform themselves into such creatures as wolves or bats; and exert command over foxes, owls, rats, mice and even moths. They can become small enough to slip beneath the crack of a door; and finally, they can filter in and out of anywhere by reducing themselves to a mere mist, or disintegrating temporarily into particles of elemental dust resembling rays of moonlight. As a link to witchcraft, vampires also can control such elements as storms, hail, thunder and fog, up to a limited range.

To offset these noteworthy advantages, vampires, like many

evil things, lose their power by daylight. They cannot effect their changes between sunrise and sunset, except at high noon. They can rest only in the shelter of their graves, or coffin-homes; and their return there may be blocked by running water, or the flow of a tide. Vampires cannot enter a house unless invited by someone living there; but once inside, they can go and return at will. A branch of wild rose on a coffin prevents a vampire from leaving it and they are allergic to the buckthorn and laurel, while garlic is universally recognized as a vampire repellent.

Vampires, like other demons, shrink from all sacred objects and relics. The fragrance of incense used in religious ceremonies may also render them powerless. Forces of evil, being negative, just can't win out over forces of good, which are positive. That, at least, is the theory, and it is a sound one inasmuch as it is first necessary to admit that good exists in order to be bad.

It is claimed that a prowling vampire can be destroyed by being shot in the heart with a silver bullet, except in the light of the full moon, which will restore and double the vampire's vigor. But the stake through the heart is a standard remedy, provided that it is driven with a single blow. Choice of wood is also important, with aspen, maple, hawthorn and buckthorn regarded among the best.

Decapitation is another recommended method and one that some regard as the best. The act should be done with the sharp edge of a grave digger's spade rather than with a sword or other such implement. Often, two methods are used together, such as driving the stake and chopping off the head. This gives double assurance that the task has been done. Sometimes, the vampire screams like a living person while these processes are under way, but that may be mere deception, calculated to make the destroyers desist. Occasionally, vampires who have prowled for a century or more and have been sparing in their blood feasts, are apt to crumble into dust almost immediately. In that case, there is no doubt that they have been destroyed, but the surest method is by using fire; for once a vampire's body has been burned to ashes, the fiend has nothing left in which to prowl.

There are other ways to become a vampire besides having been bitten by one. People of extremely evil or malevolent natures have a good chance of automatically becoming vampires, just like witches and warlocks. In fact, some students of the subject incline to the opinion that witch burning is not just a disposal of a witch of the past, but a precaution against a vampire of the future. Tradition has it that suicides are very apt to become vampires; and the same rule may apply to some persons who die by unexpected violence. The inference in both cases is that the persons involved should have normally lived longer than they did and therefore crossed over into a state of undead.

Other traditional ways whereby vampires may be engendered is for a cat to approach or spring across a body before it has been buried; and the same may apply if a bird flies over the body. Here, the link with witchcraft is definite indeed, as witches often have cats as familiars, or can turn themselves into cats or birds as well. Hence a cat or bird in the presence of a corpse is probable proof that a witch is at work, hoping to engender a vampire by spellbinding the person's body and soul together. A cat, however, might even be the Devil in disguise, come to claim its own.

Rather than theorize further on such possibilities, it is preferable to consider them in the light of actual reports on vampires and their insidious activities. These will be treated in detail in the next chapter, taking a variety of cases in somewhat chronological order. These, however, simply represent highlights of vampirism over the years. Many others that were equally spectacular have been omitted purely because they might prove redundant; while some that were very well-attested fall into routine categories. The important point to keep in mind is that the samplings given represent only a fractional percentage of those available, making vampires and vampirism a comprehensive subject in its own right.

11
The Kiss of Death

In areas where belief in vampires was strongest, their very prevalence reduced them to the commonplace. People avoided vampires or sought to destroy them much as they would gather crops or go to war. But as cases developed beyond the boundaries of such lands as Transylvania, they created so much stir that detailed reports began to be demanded. One of the earliest of such documented accounts, was the case of the Vampire of Breslau, a suicide victim. The facts were given by a famous English philosopher, Dr. Henry More, in 1653.

Dr. More claimed that on September 20, 1591, a shoemaker living in Breslau, Germany, went out in the garden and cut his throat with his shoemaker's knife. Members of his family found the body and covered up the suicide by attributing his death to apoplexy. He was given an honorable funeral two days later, but during the succeeding weeks, whispers began to grow into loud rumors that the shoemaker had committed suicide.

Apparently, these rumors were started by people who thought that they had seen the shoemaker's ghost. The family boldly denied the suicide charge and there was no way of proving it except by exhuming the body, which they refused to allow. Subsequently, the specter began to appear in earnest, awakening some people with frightful visions of the dead shoemaker and attacking others in a bodily form that was equally recognizable. So violent were the actions of this incredible being, that men who became his targets began sitting up at nights in dining rooms, with candles lighted, seeking protection in one another's company.

Yet the living dead man even attacked members of such groups, as well as isolated individuals. In panic, people were deserting the houses where such things were reported and a wave of terror swept Breslau. As a result, the city fathers overrode the family's protests and disinterred the body on April 18, 1592. Seven months underground had actually improved its condition — it was entire, the joints and limbs were flexible, there was no ill odor except that of the grave clothes, which had gone musty. Close inspection disclosed the throat wound that the family had denied, but the body was far too robust for the amount of blood it must have lost.

The body was kept on view for the next week, but reports of the grim specter continued, so the authorities decided to lay the dead shoemaker's ghost along with his body by burying the latter beneath a gallows, but that remedy fell flat. The phantom resumed operations, and in true vampire fashion again bodily attacked people, but more violently than ever. This time, members of the dead man's family and their household were targets, and his widow personally begged the officials to take more stringent action, which they did.

On May 7, 1592, the body was again exhumed and found to have swollen surprisingly during the past two weeks. It was promptly dismembered and the heart, when removed, was found to be as fresh and entire as that of a newly-killed calf. The various parts were consigned to a funeral pyre and reduced to ashes that were scattered on the River Oder. With that, as was to be expected, the vampire visitations ended; but only so far as the suicide shoemaker was concerned.

In his family household was a maidservant who had been the object of one of the vampire's later and more violent attacks. She happened to die not long afterward and, eight days later, she reappeared in physical form and attacked another servant. On another appearance, this new vampire snatched a child from its cradle, but was driven off by a vigilant nurse. From then on, the vampire maid became more cunning, appearing and tormenting people not just in her own bodily form, but as a cat, a dog and a goat. Her body was duly exhumed and burned, putting an end to the new nuisance.

The indication here is that the maidservant was the only one of the vampire shoemaker's victims who died soon enough to become a vampire herself. Her rapidly acquired ability to transform herself into a variety of physical shapes was definite evidence that she belonged in the vampire category.

Another case from a small town near Breslau, also recorded by the industrious Dr. More, involved an alderman of a somewhat profane character and therefore good vampire timber. Added to that, the circumstances of his death were of a highly significant nature.

While fixing a shoe on a horse, the alderman received an unexpected kick that proved fatal. Such an accidental death was bad enough, but even worse, as he was gasping his last earthly breath in a fit of delirium, the casement window burst open and a huge black cat sprang in upon his bed and clawed at his face as though eager to carry him off as prey; then, just as suddenly, the cat was gone. On the day of the funeral, a great tempest arose, but abated as soon as the alderman's body was buried. That portent foretold further ill.

Soon, the whole town began to be disturbed by what seemed to be a fiend incarnate, which spoke to many frightened people in a voice they recognized as the deceased alderman's. He was heard to stride about houses that he had often entered during life, so forcibly that he shook the walls and made the windows flash with light. One troubled burgher going outdoors the next morning found hoof marks in the snow that were so unusual that they could have been the Devil's own.

The alderman's own house received a due share of such attention. The town watchman reported a great stir there every night, with horses kicking their stalls apart, breaking loose and biting one another. Both the local parson and his wife were attacked by the spectral alderman, and he was also recognized by their maid, whom he assaulted.

Dozens of other reported portentous events gave validity to the vampire rumors, including the appearance of blue lights about candle flames prior to the vampire's approach, the transforming of bowls of milk into blood and the uprooting of posts too heavy for two men to lift. Children were snatched from their cradles and old men were strangled. Most phenomenal of all, the alderman's own tombstone was tilted from place, revealing openings the size of mouse holes extending clear down to his coffin; and whenever people filled these, they were mysteriously reopened by the next morning.

After nearly six months of this, the grave was opened and the alderman's body was found fresher than at the time of his death. When it was dismembered for burning, the blood literally spurted from it and the funeral pyre required more than two hundred huge logs to complete the cremation. But it was worth it, for the vampire disturbances immediately ended.

Around 1720, the entire village of Haidam, Hungary, was subjected to a mass attack by vampires, all following a pattern so insidious that they might have spread indefinitely, but for the vigilance of a soldier who happened to be quartered at a farmhouse in the town. He became friendly with several persons who had their meals there and one night, as they were sitting down to dinner, an elderly stranger entered and took his place in a chair beside the farmer, whom he watched steadily and intently.

The stranger did not eat, which was not exactly surprising, for neither did anyone else, except the soldier. Nor did anyone talk, until the obviously unwanted visitor silently went on his way. Even then, conversation was hushed and any mention of the incident was avoided, so the soldier waited until morning to ask questions. By then, they were unnecessary. The farmer had been found dead in his bed and everyone was blurting out the horrendous fact that the singular guest was none other than the farmer's father, who had been dead some years and had come to warn his son that his own death was soon due.

To the soldier this was more than a mere ghostly visitation, for the stranger had looked as solid as everyone else around the table, and from the way they all recognized him, the soldier gathered that they had seen him on other occasions. So the soldier reported the case to some officers, who relayed it to the commanding general, who, in turn made a prompt investigation. All that the soldier had reported was confirmed; a notary took affidavits from the witnesses; and an army surgeon opened the grave of the farmer's father to make sure that the body was really there.

It not only was there, it was in fresh condition after all those years, looking exactly as the witnesses had described it. The case was classed a vampirism and the investigators began checking on how often and how far the vampire had roamed. To their astonishment, they began hearing more about vampires than victims, for it was an accepted routine around Haidam for dead relatives to appear in the flesh and throw a hush over a family, during an evening meal. Though well spaced, these cases ran into the dozens, usually bringing such baleful omens that each family kept its worry to itself.

One man who had been buried more than sixteen years had caused the death of two of his sons during his bloodthirsty forays. Another, who had been in the grave for thirty years, had appeared three times at the family board, attacking first his brother, the next time one of his sons, and finally a farm servant, departing with surprising speed after biting the victim's neck and draining his blood. All three had died almost immediately, but witnesses had been too horrified to report the cause of the deaths.

Whether the vampires were acting in concert, or simply following accepted vampire procedure, it was evident that an epidemic was in the making, so all suspected bodies were exhumed including those of victims who could have acquired the vampire taint. All those who had been seen most often after death were still ruddy, regardless of how long they had been entombed; so they, as well as some others, were given the spike and decapitation treatment. Vampirism was thus stamped out in Haidam and a full first-hand report was filed at the University of Fribourg, where it may still be available.

One unusual case where a vampire failed to return to its grave was reported from the Moravian village of Liebava, where the populace was so terrified by a bloodthirsty rover that they brought in a Hungarian investigator to curb the outrage. The vampire was supposedly a prominent, but unscrupulous citizen who had died a few years before and was now literally bleeding townsfolk in death as he had done financially in life. The investigator, perhaps to avoid complications with relatives of the deceased, stationed himself nightly in the high belfry of the church, so he could watch the graveyard from which the vampire reportedly came.

His vigil paid off handsomely. One night, he saw a figure stalk from the suspected tomb, but it lacked the shroud and winding sheet in which the corpse had been buried. So as soon as the ominous figure had moved off through the village, the investigator descended from his vantage spot and approached the tomb. Though the coffin was below ground, with no sign of the earth being disturbed, the gruesome garments were lying on the grave itself, having been left there by the vampire, so that he could roam in the guise of the living, rather than the dead.

The investigator carried this funereal evidence back up to the belltower and watched until the vampire returned. As he expected, the undead prowler showed all the cunning of his ilk. Discovering that his grave clothes were gone, he sensed immediately where they had been taken and shouted up to the belfry, demanding their return. The investigator responded by flaunting the musty garments and challenging their owner to come and get them. The harangue brought witnesses to the scene, where they gazed in horror at the figure they recognized as a living dead man, ferociously climbing the steep tower steps to reclaim his stolen garb.

Note again how the lore and law of vampirism was evidencing itself in this case. This vampire, as with others just cited, was attracted to places it had known in life, such as the man's own home and other houses where he had been welcome. Nor was it difficult for it to be invited into other homesteads by unsuspecting persons. But it could never have invaded a totally unfamiliar place, least of all the tower of a church, without express command, which it gained in this instance.

Moreover, once it had reached the top, the vampire, by dint of its superhuman strength, could have easily overpowered the man who had so recklessly challenged it. Hence the people below were sure that the investigator was doomed to become another victim of the vampire; but he fortunately knew the ways of such creatures — their line of attack was invariably direct. So, when the vampire arrived, he countered by flinging the winding sheet and other graveyard garb over its head and shoulders. While it was still entangled, he managed to trip it and send it plunging headlong to the bottom of the stairway, which was as steep as the average ladder.

The jolt was enough to immobilize even a body that was merely reanimated and therefore insensible to pain; at least long enough for the sexton to arrive with a sharp-bladed spade and sever the creature's neck. The body was identified as that of the suspected vampire; and the tomb, when opened, proved to be empty.

The fact that reports of vampires have lessened through the years does not necessarily mean that they can be shrugged off to imagination and superstition. It could well be that the stringent counter-measures taken in the days when they were really rampant was responsible for their sharp reduction in number.

One of the most remarkable of modern cases was the Vampire of Croglin Grange, described in detail by Augustus Hare, who wrote many European guide books during the Victorian Era and was a most unlikely person to indulge in fancy. Hare gained the account directly from the people most involved in it — a woman whom we will call Sylvia and her two brothers, members of a wealthy family that Hare purposely did not name, though he gave the locale of their adventure.

Sylvia and her brothers rented a staid old English mansion called Croglin Grange, that had a large veranda fronting on a terrace, and grounds sweeping downward to an ancient church in a hollow, with a fine view of the distant countryside beyond. They spent an enjoyable winter there and it was not until the following summer that a shocking experience occurred.

One very hot night, they dined on the veranda and afterward, Sylvia went to her room, which overlooked the terrace. From her bed, she studied a scene illuminated by the rising moon, until she noted two strange lights that flickered from a fringe of trees between the lawn and the churchyard. Soon, they emerged, surrounded by a dark shape that seemingly approached the house, for it steadily increased in size except when it was lost momentarily in some of the long, dark shadows that streaked the moonlit lawn.

Frightened as the thing loomed to human size, Sylvia was about to start for the door to the hallway, which was close to the window, intending to call her brothers, when the shape was at the window itself, glaring in at her with eyes that blazed from a horribly grotesque visage and scratching at the pane with clawlike hands. Fortunately, Sylvia had bolted the window as well as the door, so she darted back to bed, to get farther away from the menacing creature, thinking that once it found it could not enter, it would soon go away.

Instead, the scratching turned into a pecking sound and Sylvia suddenly realized that the monstrous menace was picking away the lead that held the window pane. Too scared to scream, she heard the glass drop loose and saw a bony claw come through and draw the bolt. The window was open and accompanied by a surge of the cool night air. In an instant, the creature was upon her, twisting her hair with its long-nailed claws and drawing her head over the side of the bed, so that her face met the gleam of those ruddy eyes. Even worse was the sight of the creature's mouth, spread in a lipless smile which accentuated the long, sharp teeth that glistened like fangs in the moonlight. Suddenly, those teeth were at Sylvia's throat, biting with a razorlike champ that roused her from her petrified state. The scream she gave was far more piercing than any the vampire itself might have uttered, even if it had paused in the midst of its gory feast.

Only it wouldn't have paused, if Sylvia's brothers hadn't heard her shrieks. They reached her door and beat it down with hammer, tongs and poker, while Sylvia was still howling for aid and the vampire was making the most of his gruesome opportunity.

By the time Sylvia's brothers broke into the room, the vampire was on its way out through the open window. While one brother looked after Sylvia the other chased the monster over the lawn, where it finally escaped by tremendous leaps that carried it past the trees into the churchyard, where it disappeared. The brothers sent for a doctor, who treated Sylvia's badly lacerated throat and decided that she must have been the victim of some local lunatic. But a check proved that nobody of that sort was loose, so Sylvia's brothers settled the problem by closing Croglin Grange and taking her to Switzerland for the rest of the year.

There, Sylvia insisted that they return to Croglin Grange, as they had a long term lease on the place. So they did and passed an uneventful, and therefore happy, winter, — probably because Sylvia's brothers slept constantly in an opposite room with loaded pistols beneath their pillows, ready for the menace only she and they believed was real.

On a night in March it returned. Scratches at the window awakened Sylvia and she saw the same glaring, monstrous face staring in at her. Her timely shrieks brought her brothers out to the veranda, to intercept the hideous creature's flight. One of their pistol shots clipped the monster in a leg, but it still managed to hobble across a wall beyond the trees and disappear into the churchyard.

The next day, Sylvia's brothers summoned all the neighbors, who willingly agreed to open a long forgotten vault, into which the monster could have gone. They found it full of coffins, all tossed about with horribly mangled skeletons — except for one. In that box, brown and withered, they found the hideous creature that had attacked Sylvia, bearing the mark of a bullet that her brother had fired. So they burned the mummified monster and ended the menace of Croglin Grange.

Among American vampires, an outstanding case was reported in a small town north of San Francisco, late in November, 1891. Earlier that month, a family named Walsingham had moved into a farm house near a river and soon things began to happen in the place. The doorbell rang at odd hours, with no one about to ring it; doors themselves were slammed; and even some of the furniture was tossed about. Being newcomers, the Walsinghams assumed that they were simply victims of pranks and began watching for the perpetrators.

This continued for three weeks, during which the disturbances were amplified by horrible shrieks and wails that came from remote portions of the house and, on occasion, from outdoors. That only made Mr. and Mrs. Walsingham and their two daughters all the more determined to find the responsible parties; but every time they completed a futile search of the upstairs rooms, they were taunted by ghoulish, unearthly laughter.

Still, there was no direct physical threat, so the Walsinghams stayed on, as people often do in the face of poltergeist disturbances, which these appeared to be. But at the end of the third week, the action suddenly graduated to vampire status. One of the Walsingham daughters was seated in front of a mirror, arranging her hair, when she heard someone enter the room behind her and felt a hand laid lightly on her shoulder. She lowered her arms and tilted her head as she looked into the mirror, expecting to see her mother or her sister. Instead, the mirror showed only the reflection of the empty room behind her!

No sign of a face, nor even of the hand that right then was sliding from the girl's shoulder, down past her elbow, where it took a powerful clamp on her forearm. This time, she looked directly downward, instead of in the mirror, and to her horror she saw a man's brawny hand clutching her arm and digging its long, bony fingers into her flesh. She saw the man's arm as well, but not the rest of his figure nor his face, for by then, she was wrenching frantically in the other direction, trying to get free from the hideous embrace that she felt was coming next.

The girl's wild screams brought her mother and sister on the run. As she heard them coming, she either managed to disengage herself from the monster's grip, or for some reason, her attacker suddenly relinquished his hold. But as she reached the door to warn her mother and sister away from the menace, they greeted her with expressions of complete astonishment. Turning in the direction of their gaze, her fright turned to equal bewilderment. The room was empty!

Somehow the eerie visitor had gone as uncannily as it had come, but there was no doubt as to its reality. The girl's arm still hurt from the crushing grip and the marks of fingers and scratches from the nails were plainly visible. After hearing her story, the others decided that it was time to call in the neighbors, which they did; and all that night, they were alert in case the entity showed itself again, but nothing occurred.

The next evening, however, when the Walsinghams and some of their guests were seated around the dinner table, they heard a weird, moaning sound apparently coming from the room directly above. As they kept looking up, expecting it to recur, something dripped down from the ceiling and spattered on the tablecloth, where it gradually spread into a crimson blot, resembling blood. Mr. Walsingham and other men rushed to the upstairs room, but found it empty, with no clue to the source of the bloody drip.

Yet, while they searched, the drip continued in the room below and when it finally ceased, it was still as much a mystery as when it started. The next day, the authorities were summoned and the huge stain on the tablecloth was analyzed by chemists who pronounced it to be human blood. That was enough for the Walsinghams; they packed up and left that same day.

Note how these indications of a modern vampire fitted with the accepted lore. A physical form was finally present, as is always the case with vampires; but its reflection could not be seen in the mirror — another sure sign; and the dripping blood was equally significant. Furthermore, there was a sequel to this case that helped to corroborate the evidence of vampirism.

Among the hundreds of curiousity seekers who came to see the Walsingham house was one man who decided to stay there overnight and see what happened. He brought a lamp with him and started a fire in the fireplace; but almost immediately, weird noises began and the fire was smothered and its embers scattered by unseen hands, while the lamp was extinguished and broken. While the man was trying to find his way out in the dark, powerful hands seized him and choked and battered him until he blacked out.

In the morning, the self-appointed investigator was found unconscious, with finger marks and scratches on his neck and throat, duplicating the experience of Walsingham's daughter, only worse. This man was hospitalized for weeks, apparently having suffered a great loss of blood, though his body showed no gashes or other severe wounds, except those throat scratches, which could have covered incisions from a vampire's teeth.

According to report, the deserted house later burned down. There was no mention of arson, but if it happened to be suspected, there was still a question whether the fire was set by human or inhuman hands. Whether or not the vampire burned up with it was also unanswered.

Perhaps these weird occurrences can best be summed in the words of the famous actor, Bela Lugosi, who appeared in the role of the granddaddy of all vampires, Count Dracula, on the stage, and later, in films. Always, after the final curtain, he returned on stage, still in his Dracula makeup, to tell the audience that after all, it was just a play and to wish them all a pleasant goodnight; to which he added in sepulchral tones:

"But remember — such things do happen!"

12
Lycanthropy: Werewolves and Their Kin

The subjects of werewolves and vampires are so closely related in the public's mind that they are often regarded as interchangeable, which they are not; indeed, far from it. Both are associated with witchcraft, but from there on, the line of demarcation is very sharp indeed.

While the vampire is supposedly a corpse that is animated or enlivened by the undead entity that formerly controlled it, a werewolf is a living person plagued by the unhappy faculty of frequently changing his bodily form from that of a man into a wolf, and vice versa. Such a change may be voluntary or involuntary; and while usually of a temporary nature, it may sometimes become permanent.

Confusion between vampires and werewolves is due partly to the fact that a vampire reputedly has the power of transforming itself into a wolf; hence it could easily be mistaken for a werewolf while in such a transitory state. And since both are vicious and bloodthirsty, their actions might also be similar.

However, vampires seldom retain their lupine shapes very long, and are more apt to dissolve into mist or moonbeams when bound upon their nefarious missions, assuming their human forms later. Conversely, werewolves avoid frequent or hurried changes, unless they are being pursued; and they are said to revert to human form automatically if injured — a decided handicap to say the least. In all, werewolves are far more vulnerable than vampires, but that does not make them any more human. Where vampires usually are only out for blood, werewolves like to tear people apart and devour them completely. You're not likely to have a second chance to meet a werewolf.

Another distinctive feature to remember is that a person can be transformed by witchery into a wolf, instead of some other animal; and in that case, the change remains immutable until the spell is broken, as was described in the legend of Sir Marrok.

Werewolves, of course, are hardly benign, though they might fool you by pretending to be. In contrast, a person transformed into a wolf by witchcraft might become cantakerous indeed, through sheer frustration. Finally, real wolves can be bad enough, according to the authors of *Malleus Maleficarum*, who declared in 1486: "There is a great power in the eyes and this appears even in natural things. For if a wolf see a man first, the man is struck dumb."

To explain why that happened, the authors cited the long-established legend of a fabled monster called the *basilisk*, generally classed as a species of dragon.

> *If a basilisk sees a man first, its glance is fatal, but if he sees it first, he may be able to kill it. The reason a basilisk can kill a man by its glare is that when it sees him, its anger sets in motion a terrible poison throughout its body, which it darts from its eyes, infusing the air with deadly venom. Thus the man breathes in the infected atmosphere and is overpowered and dies.*
>
> *But when the basilisk is first seen by the man, who wishes to kill it, he should be supplied with mirrors; and the creature, seeing itself in the mirrors, darts poison toward its reflection, which recoils upon the basilisk and causes it to die.*

Having treated the situation so convincingly and scientifically, the authors tied it in with their pet theme that witches, too, could fascinate or bind people with a mere glance; and from that, they backtracked to the question of wolves and how witchcraft could apply in their case:

> *There is a question about wolves, which sometimes snatch people out of their houses and eat them and run about so craftily that they cannot be hurt or captured. This sometimes has a natural cause; but it can also be due to a glamor effected by witches. . . .*
>
> *As to whether they are real wolves, or devils appearing in that form, we say that they are real wolves, but that they are possessed by devils, which may happen without the operation of witches — but in another way, may be an illusion caused by witches.*
>
> *For it is told of a man who thought that he was turned into a wolf and at times went into hiding among caves. Though he remained there constantly immobile, he believed that he was a wolf that went about devouring children. The Devil, having possessed a wolf, was actually doing this, but the man mistakenly thought that he was prowling while asleep.*
>
> *So long was he thus out of his right mind that he was eventually found raving in the woods. The Devil delights in things of this sort, which proves that it was the Devil who caused the illusion of the old pagans who believed that men and women were changed into beasts.*

In these opinions, the authors of *Malleus Maleficarum* were for once ahead of their time, at least to a noteworthy degree. Reginald Scot, the hard-headed skeptic of a century later, left the Devil out of it and classed such imaginary transformations as a disease called Lycanthropy, which for a while was attributed to the bite of a mad wolf. But many people still believed that werewolves were real, and with good reason — the gruesome deeds charged to suspected werewolves transcended anything human.

In 1521, a man traveling through the French department of Jura, near the Swiss border, was attacked by a ferocious wolf, but managed to beat it off and wound it. Following its bloody trail, he reached a lonely cottage where a woman was giving first aid to her husband, a peasant named Michel Verdun, who had been badly injured. Suspicious, the traveler reported the occurrence to the authorities in the town of Poligny, who were prompt to investigate because at intervals, several persons, including children, had been killed and horribly mangled by wolves that had shown almost human cunning.

Under questioning, Michel Verdun confessed that he was a werewolf and that he had initiated a shepherd named Pierre Bourgot into the ways and wiles of such dreadful creatures. By smearing themselves with two types of ointment provided by a familiar demon, they were able to change themselves into wolves and back again, in the meantime tearing out the throats of human beings, lapping up their blood and sometimes devouring their bodies.

Bourgot was tortured into corroborating Verdun's confession and added some juicy details of his own. Between them, they implicated another peasant, Philibert Mentot, who made similar admissions. All three described how their hands and feet would become hairy and turn into paws. When the transformation was complete, they would race across the countryside at such speed that it was more fun to be wolves than men. Eventually they found themselves running, living and mating with the wolf pack for extended periods.

From then on, the Jura district became a notorious habitat of the *loup-garou*, as the French termed a werewolf. By 1573, the menace was so great that a proclamation was issued calling upon the peasantry to turn out and pursue, bind and kill all such horrendous creatures. They finally caught up with a fiendish hermit named Gilles Garnier, who lived near the town of Dole, and who admitted attacking four children, with intent of killing, dismembering and devouring them.

Twice, Garnier had been completely successful; he even described how, in the shape of a wolf, he had used his clawed paws and sharp fangs to eat his victims piecemeal, reserving portions for later repasts. Once, after he had seized a small girl, some men came to her rescue and he was forced to drop his prey and lope away as a *loup-garou*. On another occasion, he was so eager for the kill that he couldn't wait to change into a wolf. Still in human guise, he strangled a boy, then abandoned the body when some peasants approached. Later, they identified Garnier as the killer, and he was burned forthwith.

A still more fantastic case cropped up in the same area in 1598, when a sixteen-year-old boy tried to save his younger sister from the attack of a ferocious wolf, only to have it turn on him instead. Men who rushed to the youth's aid found him dying from wounds inflicted by a knife which he himself carried, indicating that the wolf had snatched it from him and stabbed him with it. That meant that the wolf must have had hands instead of forepaws.

The men overtook the wolf and had all but killed it when it managed to flounder off into the brush. Positive that the creature was mortally wounded, they made a search for it and instead of finding a wolf, they came across the body of a half-witted woman named Perrenette Gandillon. By the equally half-witted logic of that era, the searchers rejected the idea that the wolf might have killed the woman earlier. Instead, finding Perrenette where they should have found the wolf, they decided that the two must be one and that Perrenette was a werewolf who had reverted to human form, as werewolves invariably do in death.

So they rounded up three members of the Gandillon family for such intensive questioning that soon all were implicating themselves on a variety of counts, such as raising storms by witchcraft, attending sabbats where the Devil presided as a goat, and frequently becoming werewolves by using the customary ointment. The Gandillons were fortunate in being tried by a judge who wondered if these things could really happen; so in their stupid way, they hopped about on all fours, giving appropriate howls. When they didn't turn into wolves, they blamed it on lack of ointment, but decided that it wouldn't work if they had it, as imprisonment had dulled their devil-given powers. However, their impersonations were good enough to convince the skeptical judge that they really had roved as werewolves, so he sent them to the stake.

So it continued on through the years, not only in France, but throughout Europe, up to comparatively modern times. In Portugal, a mere century or so ago, the story was told of a serving-maid who came from a mountain region and took a job with a family living in a town near Ponte de Lima. Soon afterward, a baby boy was born in the family and someone noted that the infant had a "Devil's Mark" in the form of a crescent between its shoulders. This, according to a still current superstition, meant that the child should be watched carefully whenever the moon was at that crescent phase. The new maid heard of this and told the family of a method used by mountain-folk to counteract such evil. That was to smear the mark with the blood of a white pigeon and place the child on a hillside where its body would be exposed to the glow of the new moon, which would efface the sinister mark.

That was done, but the father of the child, fearful that some animal might molest it, remained nearby with a loaded gun. Hardly had the moon risen when he fancied he heard a child's cry and he rushed to the spot to find a huge wolf glaring from above the infant's body, with gore dripping from its snarling mouth. Too late to save the baby, the man fired point blank at the wolf, and a boy who accompanied the father, managed to strike its right forepaw with a club as it rolled over and then tried to dart away.

The dead child's throat was horribly torn and mangled; and after they carried the body back to the house, they discovered that the new maid was no longer there. Suddenly suspicious, they began a search of the woods into which the wolf had run. There, they found the maid, dying from gunshot wounds, gripping a broken right wrist. She gasped that she had been worried about the baby's safety, so she had watched from behind a tree and had seen a wolf attack it. As she rushed to the rescue, the wolf leaped away and she had received the gunshot instead. But the glare in her dying eyes was too much like the wolf's for the child's father to believe her; and she didn't live long enough to explain the broken wrist that could obviously have resulted from the stroke of the boy's club.

The maid's breast also bore the Devil's Mark and a checkup proved that werewolves had long been rampant in the district where she had lived. Apparently, she had been trying to shake off the curse, for according to an old legend, that could only be done by killing an infant and imbibing its blood.

It is much easier to become a werewolf than a vampire. The trait is said to be hereditary, but others can become werewolves by eating a wolf's brains, or drinking from the same stream as wolves. But the best way of all is by burning certain substances, particularly poppy seeds. Here, skeptics see a subtle clue to the possible explanation of werewolfery: Such fumigations produce hallucinations, causing people to think they have become wolves, or at least gained wolfish desires. The same could apply to the ointments used in such transformations; as with the so-called flying ointments, the results could be purely imaginary.

But that raises other questions: Why just werewolves? Why don't people change themselves into other dangerous creatures through sheer power of witchcraft? The answer is twofold. They don't limit themselves to wolves; and they do change themselves into other creatures. But they follow a consistent pattern. Whatever bestial guise is assumed through witchcraft, it invariably combines strength with cunning to a degree that the average human not only fears, but envies. Through much of Europe, the wolf took top rating in that category. A wolf howl at night could scare even the folk who dwelt in marble halls; while those who starved in hovels could very well wish that they were out howling with the wolf-pack and getting their share of whatever it was, if only to help scare those who dwelt in marble halls.

But in the more northern climes, witches and warlocks were supposed to assume the shape of bears, which were more formidable than wolves and also showed remarkable intelligence. In India and Malaysia, were-tigers were regarded as the products of fiendish witchcraft that preyed on humans in inhuman style. In Japan, the *ninko,* or man-fox, made up in craftiness for what it lacked in size. In Africa, leopards and hyenas were the equivalent of European werewolves; and occasionally crocodiles were granted a similar status.

The Human Leopard Society, which flourished in the former British colony of Sierra Leone, was one of the most remarkable animal cults on record. It was used by witch doctors to extort tribute from the wealthier members of the native villages, but with a promise of profitable return that developed into a fantastic racket. The witch doctor began by providing a client with a *borfima,* or "medicine bag," which contained various gruesome ingredients, the most important being human fat and blood.

The fortunate owner of a borfima could count on it to bring him riches and power, to protect him in a colonial court, and to implement any curses or misfortunes that he wished upon his enemies. Naturally, borfimas were costly, but worth their price when they functioned as expected. Contrarily, when they failed, which they often did, customers wanted their money back. That wasn't possible with a borfima, an illegal product to begin with; but in buying it, the purchaser automatically gained membership in the Human Leopard Society, which solved the problem.

At the next meeting, in a secret rendezvous deep in the African bush, the principal witch doctor told disgruntled members that the parent borfima, from which theirs had been taken, needed to be freshly bloodied and supplied with enough human fat to restore its potency. That done, their individual borfimas could be replenished from the main source. They then chose a suitable victim — often a member of one of their own families — and decoyed him to his doom. Chosen members of the cult garbed themselves in leopard skins, sneaked up on their quarry and killed him with three-pronged knives designed to resemble leopard's claws.

This was not done to lull the unsuspecting victim, who by then not only suspected something, but knew that he wasn't going to come out of it alive enough to tell. It was designed to mislead any witnesses, by making them think that leopards, not people, had been responsible for the victim's death, in case the killers were unable to carry away their prey. Otherwise, they took the body to the meeting place, added its blood and fat to the parent borfima and carved up what was left and ate it, thus topping off the evening in true cannibalistic style.

Why they did this doesn't matter. It may have been a reversion to an ancient rite. It could have been an effort to outdo one another in bravado. Maybe they thought they were digesting some of the virility of the victim whose body they devoured. Maybe they were just crazy enough to think they were human leopards. Or they could have felt that it did increase the potency of their individual borfimas that were finally dished out from the main mess. Anyway, the cult members were willing to go along with the presiding witch doctors until they saw how well the new "medicine" worked.

If it worked well for most of the members, fine; it not, it merely meant another sacrificial rite to replenish the parent borfima still further. What the human leopards didn't realize was that they, in their way, were almost as badly hooked as their victims. Once in the clutches of the cult, there was no escaping it; and as it grew in size and power, the increase in deaths attributed to leopards invariably roused the suspicions of the authorities. From 1903 to 1912, 17 cases were tried before a circuit court, involving 186 suspects charged with murder, 87 of whom were convicted and sentenced to death as human leopards.

Then, the cracking of a sensational case against the Human Leopard Society produced leads to some 30 murders so far overlooked, involving nearly 400 suspects. Though many were released due to lack of corroborative evidence, the power of the Human Leopard Society apparently was broken, along with that of an offshoot known as the Human Alligator Society, whose members lurked near streams, snugly clad in alligator hides. But after several years, the outrages of these sinister societies flared anew, spreading from Sierra Leone to Nigeria; and again they were curtailed, continuing only intermittently until the time of World War II.

Then the hideous slayings were renewed with new fury, with reported cases averaging one a week over a two-year period ending early in 1948, when 73 suspected human leopards were held on murder charges; and of these, 39 were found guilty and executed.

Fakery of this sort, far from discrediting werewolves and their ilk, may be taken as *prima facie* evidence of their existence, in accordance with an oft-quoted claim that unless something is real to start with, it can't be counterfeited. Unquestionably, many members of the Sierra Leone cult must have believed that their leaders could actually transform themselves into leopards and that they, the followers, were being taught the trade by putting on their masquerade.

In many lands far from Sierra Leone, witch doctors were going through such transformations regularly, without organizing cults to help. A vivid account of such witchcraft was reported in 1948, from the state of Mato Grosso in Brazil. There, two Brazilian officers were sent to investigate the murder of the head man of a village on the Bolivian border, only to find that the natives blamed it on a huge jaguar that roamed the area at nights and was responsible for other previous deaths. But the head man happened to be the village's best hunter as well, so by all rights, he should have slain the jaguar, rather than vice versa. By jungle logic, the fact that the jaguar had won out simply verified a rumor that the dreaded beast was actually a local witch doctor, whose powers the villagers feared even more.

To confirm local superstitions, the witch doctor invariably had been absent from the village when the phantom jaguar prowled in search of anything from goats to human prey. So rather than argue with the natives, the officers decided to dispel the dual menace with the aid of a double-barreled shotgun, a weapon totally unknown in those parts. They tethered a goat near the village and attached cords to the gun, planting it so that any prowling animal would trip the triggers and receive both blasts. If that eliminated the jaguar, they could deal with the witch doctor alone, later on.

That night, the well-laid booby trap went off in perfect one-two style. The officers ran out and found the goat dead at the end of its tether, mangled by deep claw marks that could only be a jaguar's. From there, a bloody trail led off through the jungle, proving that at least one blast had crippled the jaguar. With morning, the two men tried to follow it, but the foliage proved too thick. The trail's end, however, proved closer than they expected.

Excited villagers informed the officers that the local witch doctor had returned from one of his clandestine trips so badly injured that he was practically dying in his hut. The government men went there, but were unable to talk with him before he expired because one side of his lower jaw had been practically shot away. Only a shotgun could have inflicted such a wound, and the two officers had the only shotgun within hundreds of miles.

Reports of a prowling jaguar ended with that night, which to the villagers was further proof that the animal and the witch doctor were one and the same. Thus are the legendary claims of witchcraft continually renewed.

13
The Power of the Hex

A remarkable survival of witch beliefs dating from the Middle Ages is to be found in modern times among some Pennsylvania German communities, where practitioners known as "powwow doctors" continue to use long-tested charms and remedies to offset evil spells supposedly induced by witchcraft. Such practitioners are also known as "hex doctors," as opposed to a "hex," or witch, with the term "hex" also meaning "to bewitch."

This dates from the time of Alburtus Magnus, a great German philosopher of the thirteenth century, whose scientific knowledge was so far ahead of his time that much of his work was erroneously attributed to witchcraft. He was an author of many scientific works that were highly important in their day; and in later years, his name was falsely applied to various books on witchcraft to give them a distinction which they did not deserve.

Some of these books, or the remedies which they prescribed, were brought to America by early German settlers. Almost anything that promised relief from human ills or problems was included and often combined to give them double impact. Thus medicinal roots and herbs were recommended, but so were charms and spells, the latter to such degree that it was difficult to tell which was preferable. In fact, alternate measures were often used, allowing choice on a trial and error basis.

One big problem for the early settlers was finding the roots and herbs that would be the equivalents, or serve as substitutes for those they had used in Europe. They naturally asked the Indians to look for certain trees and plants; and they found, to their surprise and delight, that the Indians, too, had discovered medicinal uses for various herbs. So they began exchanging remedies and learned, even more amazingly, that the Indian medicine men used charms and incantations for curative purposes.

To drive out the devils of disease, the Indians held ceremonies that they called "powwows," so the term was adopted by the settlers and applied to their cure-alls as well. Then, in the year 1820, John George Hohman, a powwow doctor who lived near Reading, Pennsylvania, published a compact volume which he entitled, *Powwows or Long Lost Friend*. The book consisted of "a collection of mysterious and invaluable arts and remedies for man as well as animals" and to prove its efficacy, it made this bold announcement on the second page:

> *Whoever carries this book with him is safe from all his enemies, visible or invisible; and whoever has this book with him cannot die without the holy corpse of Jesus Christ, nor drown in any water, nor burn up in any fire, nor can any unjust sentence be passed upon him. So help me.*

Following that promise came the remedies, or powwows — a few hundred in all. The following samples are in original form.

HOW TO MAKE CATTLE RETURN TO THE SAME PLACE.

Take a handful of salt, go upon your fields and make your cattle walk three times around the same stump or stone, each time keeping the same direction; that is to say, you must three times arrive at the same end of the stump or stone at which you started from, then let your cattle lick the salt from the stump or stone.

A GOOD METHOD OF DESTROYING RATS AND MICE.

Every time you bring grain into your barn, you must, in putting down the first three sheaves, repeat the following words: "Rats and mice, these three sheaves I give to you, in order that you may not destroy any of my wheat." The name of the kind of grain must also be mentioned.

TO CURE ANY EXCRESCENCE OR WEN ON A HORSE.

Take any bone which you accidentally find, for you dare not be looking for it, and rub the wen of the horse with it, always bearing in mind that it must be done in the decreasing moon, and the wen will certainly disappear. The bone however, must be replaced as it was lying before.

TO PREVENT WITCHES FROM BEWITCHING CATTLE, TO BE WRITTEN AND PLACED IN THE STABLE; AND AGAINST BAD MEN AND EVIL SPIRITS WHICH NIGHTLY TORMENT OLD AND YOUNG PEOPLE, TO BE WRITTEN AND PLACED ON THE BEDSTEAD.

"Trotter Head, I forbid thee my house and premises; I forbid thee my horse and cow-stable; I forbid thee my bedstead, that thou mayest not breathe upon me; breathe into some other house, until thou hast ascended every hill, until thou hast counted every fence post, and until thou hast crossed every water. And thus dear day may come again into my house, in the name of God the Father, the Son, and the Holy Ghost. Amen."

This will certainly protect and free all persons and animals from witchcraft.

In contrast to strictly rural remedies, Hohman offered some that should prove valuable for city folk as well, perhaps even more so today than back in Hohman's own time. These could be helpful under a variety of circumstances, including a trip to Las Vegas or an encounter with a holdup man....

FOR GAINING A LAWFUL SUIT

It reads, if anyone has to settle any just claim by way of a law suit let him take some of the largest kind of sage and write the name of the twelve apostles on the leaves, and put them in his shoes before entering the courthouse, and he shall certainly gain the suit.

TO WIN EVERY GAME ONE ENGAGES IN

Tie the heart of a bat with a red silken string to the right arm, and you will win every game at cards you play.

TO STOP BLEEDING AT ANY TIME

Write the name of the four principal waters of the whole world, flowing out of Paradise, on a paper, namely: Pison, Gihon, Hedekial and Pheat, and put it on the wound. In the first book of Moses, the second chapter, verses 11, 12, 13, you will find them. You will find this effective.

A CHARM TO BE CARRIED ABOUT THE PERSON

Carry these words about you, and nothing can hit you: Ananiah, Azariah, and Misael, blessed be the Lord, for he has redeemed us from hell, and has saved us from death, and he has redeemed us out of the fiery furnace, and has preserved us from the fiery furnace, and has preserved us even in the midst of the fire; in the same manner may it please him the Lord that there be no fire.

A CHARM TO GAIN ADVANTAGE OF A MAN OF SUPERIOR STRENGTH

I (John Doe) breathe upon thee. Three drops of blood I take from thee: the first out of thy heart, the other out of thy liver, and the third out of thy vital powers; and in this I deprive thee of thy strength and manliness.

TO PREVENT ANYONE FROM KILLING GAME

Pronounce the name, as for instance, John Doe, shoot whatever you please; shoot but hair and feathers with and what you give to poor people.

Fire extinguishers hadn't been invented in Hohman's day, but he had his own way of handling such hazards. How they would help to lower insurance rates is a question. You might ask your insurance broker to make sure, for possibly Hohman's methods have been tried and proven. His formula for preventing theft or burglary, however, is badly outdated. It's hard to picture a modern thief standing still long enough to be spellbound. In fact, you might have trouble standing still that long yourself. Things evidently moved more slowly in the old days — if they moved at all.

TO EXTINGUISH FIRE WITHOUT WATER

Write the following words on each side of a plate, and throw it into the fire, and it will be extinguished forthwith:

```
S A T O R
A R E P O
T E N E T
O P E R A
R O T A S
```

ANOTHER METHOD OF STOPPING FIRE

Our dear Sarah journeyed through the land, having a fiery hot brand in her hand. The fiery brand heats; the fiery brand sweats. Fiery brand, stop your heat; fiery brand, stop your sweat.

TO SPELLBIND THIEVES

Ye thieves, I conjure you, to be obedient like Jesus Christ, who obeyed his Heavenly Father unto the cross, and to stand without moving out of my sight, in the name of the Trinity. I command you by the power of God and the incarnation of Jesus Christ, not to move out of my sight, like Jesus Christ was standing on Jordan's stormy banks to be baptized by John. And furthermore, I conjure you, horse and rider, to stand still and not to move out of my sight, like Jesus Christ did stand when he was about to be nailed to the cross to release the fathers of the church from the bonds of hell. Ye thieves, I bind you with the same bonds with which Jesus our Lord has bound hell; and thus ye shall be bound; and the same words that bind you shall also release you.

TO RELEASE SPELLBOUND PERSONS

You horseman and footman, whom I here conjure at this time, you may pass on in the name of Jesus Christ, through the word of God and the will of Christ; ride ye now and pass.

Very nice of John George Hohman to tell you how to release those spellbound thieves, rather than have them stand around indefinitely. At least it was shorter than repeating the spellbinding formula used to stop them in their tracks. But don't think that any of his remedies worked too easily. In some instances, they had to be repeated thrice in order to work at all. Yet despite that, his *Long Lost Friend* is still selling after a century and a half. And why?

Remember that promise on page two of the original edition — that no harm would befall anyone who carried the Powwow Book? Lots of people have carried copies during these past 150 years, yet there is no recorded case where harm befell any of them. Maybe J. G. H. had something that is badly needed today. Or maybe he was just a smart opportunist, trading upon the gullibility of the people he met. Possibly, he could have been impressed by the famous Dady case of twenty-three years before the publication of his book, which we have taken almost verbatim from the York County records to show the hold that witchcraft then held.

Dr. Dady, who was a German by birth, came to this country with the Hessians during the American Revolution. Possessing a fascinating eloquence in the German language, and being very fluent in English, he was afterwards employed as a minister of the gospel by uninformed but honest Germans.

When the robe could no longer be subservient to his avaricious views, he laid it aside and assumed the character of a physician. As such he went to York County, and dwelt there among the poor inhabitants of a mountainous region where, in various artful ways, he preyed on the purses of the unwary.

Of all the numerous impositions with which his name is connected, we will mention but two. The scene of one of them is in what is now Adams County, where he dwelt; the other took place in the "barrens" of York County. The following is an account of the Adams County imposition:

Rice Williams, or rather Rainsford Rogers, a New Englander, and John Hall, a New Yorker, (both of whom had been plundering the inhabitants of the southern states by their wiles) came to the house of Clayton Chamberlain, a neighbor of Dady, in July, 1797.

On the following morning, Dady went to Chamberlain's and

had a private conversation with Williams and Hall, before breakfast. After Dady had left them, Williams asked Chamberlain whether the place was not haunted. Chamberlain answered in the negative, whereupon Williams said that it was indeed haunted — that he had been born with a veil over his face — could see spirits, and had been conducted thither, sixty miles, by a spirit. Hall attested to the truth of this. In the evening of the same day, they had another interview with Dady. Williams then told Chamberlain that if he would permit him to tarry overnight, he would show him a spirit. This being agreed to, they went into a field in the evening, and Williams drew a circle on the ground, around which he directed Hall and Chamberlain to walk in silence. A terrible screech was soon heard coming from a black ghost in the woods, at a little distance from the parties, in a direction opposite to the place where Williams stood. In a few minutes a white ghost appeared, which Williams addressed in a language those others present could not understand. The ghost replied *in the same language!* After his ghostship had gone away, Williams said that the spirit knew of a treasure which it was permitted to reveal to eleven men — they must be honest, religious and sensible, and neither horse jockeys nor Irishmen.

The intercourse between Williams and Dady now ceased to be apparent; but it was continued in private. Chamberlain, convinced of the existence of a ghost and a treasure, was easily induced to form a company, which was soon effected.

Each candidate was initiated by the receipt of a small sealed paper, containing a little yellow sand, called the "power." The candidate was to bury this "power" under the earth to the depth of one inch, and leave it there for three days and three nights, each night performing several absurd ceremonies, too obscene to be described here.

A circle, two inches in diameter, was formed in the field, and in the center was a hole six inches wide and as many deep. A captain, a lieutenant and three committee men were elected. Hall had the honor of the captaincy. The exercise was to take place around the circle. This, it was said, propitiated and strengthened the white ghost, who was opposed by the unfriendly black ghost who rejoiced in the appellation of Pompey. In the course of their nocturnal exercises they often saw the white ghost. They saw Mr. Pompey, too, but he appeared to have "his back up" — he bellowed loudly, and threw stones at them.

On the night of the 18th of August, 1797, Williams undertook to get instructions from the white ghost. It was done in the following manner: He took a sheet of clean white paper, and folded it in the form of a letter, each member breathing into it three times; this being repeated several times, and the paper laid over the hole in the center of the circle, the instructions of the ghost were obtained. The following is a short extract from the epistle written by the ghost.

Go on, and do right, and proper, and the treasure shall be yours. I am permitted to write this in the same hand I wrote in the flesh for your direction. Take care of your powers in the fear of God our protector — if not, leave the work. There is a great treasure — 4,000 pounds apiece for you. Don't trust the black one. Obey orders. Break the enchantment, which you will not do until you get an ounce of mineral dulcimer elixir; some German doctor has it. It is near, and dear, and scarce. Let the committee get it; but don't let the doctor know what you are about — he is wicked.

The above is but a small part of this precious communication. In consequence of these ghostly directions, a young man named Abraham Kephart waited, by order of the committee, on Dr. Dady. The doctor preserved his elixir in a bottle sealed with a large red seal, and buried in a heap of oats, and demanded fifteen dollars an ounce for it. Young Kephart could not afford to give so much, but gave him thirty-six dollars and three bushels of oats for three ounces of it. Yost Liner, another of these wise committeemen, gave the doctor $121 for eleven ounces of the stuff.

The company was soon increased to thirty persons, many of whom were wealthy. All these and many other men were, in the words of the indictment, "cheated and defrauded by means of certain false tokens and pretences, to wit: by means of pretended spirits, certain circles, certain brown powder, and certain compositions, called dulcimer elixir, and Deterick's mineral elixir."

But the wiles of these impostors were soon exerted in other parts. The following is an account of their proceedings in and about Shrewsbury township, in York County:

Williams intimated that he had received a call from a ghost resident in those parts, at the distance of forty miles from Dady's. Jacob Wister, one of the conspirators, was the agent of Williams on this occasion. He instituted a company of twenty-one persons, all of whom were, of course, ignorant people. The same and even more absurd ceremonies were performed by these people, and the communications of the ghost were obtained in an even more ridiculous manner than before. The communications mentioned Dr. Dady as the person from whom they should obtain the dulcimer elixir, and likewise a kind of sand which the ghost called "Asiatic sand" and which was necessary in order to give efficacy to the "powers." Ulrich Neaff, a committeeman of this company, paid Dr. Dady ninety dollars for seven-and-a-half ounces of the elixir. The elixir was put into vials, and each person who had one of them held it in his hand and shook it as he pranced round the circle; on certain occasions anointing his head with it, and afterwards, by order of the spirit, the phial was buried in the ground.

Paul Baliter, another of the committeemen, took one hundred dollars to Dr. Dady's to purchase "Asiatic sand," at three dollars an ounce. In the doctor's absence, Williams procured from the doctor's shop as much sand as the money would purchase. In this instance, Williams cheated the doctor, for he kept the spoil for himself, thereby breaking up the profitable fraternity.

Each of them now went into business for himself. Williams procured directions from *his* ghost, that each of the companies should despatch a committee to Lancaster to buy "Deterick's mineral elixir" from a physician in that place. In the meantime Williams and his wife went to Lancaster, where they prepared the elixir, which was nothing but a composition of copperas and cayenne pepper. Mrs. Williams, posing as the wife of John Huber, a German doctor, went to Dr. Rose, with a letter dated "13 miles from Newcastle, Delaware," which directed him how to sell the article. The enormity of the price aroused Dr. Rose. In a few days the delegates from the committee arrived, and purchased elixir to the amount of $740.33. When the lady came for the money, she was arrested, and the secret became known. Her husband, Williams, escaped.

A few days after the disclosures made by Mrs. Williams, an indictment was made in the Criminal Court of York County against Dr. Dady and some of his accomplices. Dr. Dady was sentenced to two years confinement in the penitentiary at Philadelphia.

That hardly seemed enough.

14
Africa: Home of Witchcraft

In tracing the history of witchcraft through the centuries, it has become increasingly apparent that once a primitive idea is projected into a civilized setting and accepted, it is impossible to estimate the incredible heights it may attain. One fallacy begets another until they are all so far out that there is no returning, except by rejecting the initial premise.

The best way to strike a balance between fact and fantasy is to consider witchcraft in a natural setting where it has enjoyed a steady, understandable growth, enabling it to reach its most lavish and most highly developed form. That is throughout the continent of Africa, particularly in the tropical regions. There, animism, the belief that natural objects have souls or spirits which can exist in or apart from their physical form, was predominant. That was logical enough, as the prevalence of wild and dangerous animals along with unexplainable diseases, plus floods, droughts and other phenomena, could all be blamed on spirits.

Not that those things didn't happen elsewhere. They are experienced so often in America that insurance companies refer to them as "Acts of God" and refuse to pay off on them, as the fine print of some of your insurance policies may show. But in the Africa of the not-so-distant-past, they blamed such catastrophes on spirits and brought in the witch doctors to handle them.

In Central Africa, a type of general practitioner among witch doctors is known as a *nganga*. He makes a great show of divining past, present and future by casting "bones" that are commonly termed *hakata*, in order to interpret the way they fall. The hakata vary in design and material from split seeds, the size of dice, to actual bones. There may be as many as a dozen, bearing figures representing such creatures as an eagle, turtle, snake, crocodile, leopard, lion, along with other symbols of less obvious significance.

The nganga tosses these and reads their meaning, according to whether the marks are up or down; but sometimes his throws are too frequent or too rapid for anyone else to follow, so anyone consulting him must take his word for whatever the hakata tell him. Usually, there is nothing remarkable about this; but a British physician, Frederick Kaigh, who visited Central Africa in the 1930's, describes an instance where the bones seemingly came "alive" while the nganga who threw them was in a trance state. Two of the hakata stood on end and stayed there, while another, bearing the crocodile symbol of death, rose and then fell back. All were flat and motionless when the nganga snapped from his trance; from the crocodile's behavior, he decided that Dr. Kaigh was due for a close call with death. That proved true when his car tumbled from a mountain road a week later, though he escaped with only minor injuries.

What caused the bones to come alive in this unusual case? Threads? Magnets? Hypnotism? The most plausible answer would have to be threads, due to a special detail in Kaigh's eyewitness report: Lokanzi, the witch doctor, first smoothed a circle in the earth, then leveled it with sand from a bag he carried. That sand could very well have concealed the threads that made the hakata behave as they did. To a degree, this feat of close-up wizardry was reminiscent of a more spectacular demonstration described by a famous American magician, Samri Baldwin, who visited British Bechuanaland (now the Republic of Botswana) a half century earlier.

There, the witch doctor of a Mashona village conducted Baldwin to the bank of a small river and picked up a light log that had broken from an overhanging tree bough. The native wizard tossed the log into the river where it floated rapidly downstream until he ordered it to stop, which it did. Considering that it could have struck a shoal, Baldwin was not overly surprised; but when the Mashona wizard beckoned it to come upstream and it obeyed, that was something else again. Not only that, it stopped again, then sank entirely from sight, only to surface suddenly — all according to the witch doctor's commands. It resumed its course upstream at his direction, pausing, diving, and once jumping nearly a foot from the water. Finally, as it neared the river bank, the witch doctor waded out to meet it, brought it ashore and handed it to Baldwin for his amazed inspection.

The incident took place toward dusk and all that night Professor Baldwin pondered over the near miracle. The next day, he showed the witch doctor some feats of American wizardry so astounding that the nganga offered to swap secrets. Thus, Baldwin learned, and later revealed, the mystery of the obedient log. Though apparently lying carelessly upon the river bank, it was actually rigged for business, with two thin cords of fiber from an African plant attached to it, each about sixty feet long. Because these fibers were of the same color as the grassy bank, they escaped notice when the witch doctor threw the log into the stream, which was muddy enough to hide the cords as they were paid out by an accomplice hidden in the brush. Thanks to the dusk, the witch doctor's assistant remained unseen as he manipulated the cords to produce the desired results. When the nganga waded out and seized the animated log, he had only to detach the fiber cords and the riddle was complete.

These two cases have been cited because they so clearly emphasize the African witch doctor's perpetual purpose — to prove that all objects can be animated by a spirit force that he has the ability to summon. In commenting upon his experience with the Mashona witch doctor, Professor Baldwin, as an American stage magician, made this pointed summary:

> *I could not, however, make him understand that my performances were given simply with the idea of entertaining the public. His deceptions were given purely with the view of making his tribal comrades have an implicit belief in his supernatural powers; and he could not comprehend how any person could produce work of that character, unless it was to make others believe that it was not mere trickery, but could only be produced by individuals of the nature of a demi-god.*

Fifty years later, Dr. Kaigh, expanding on that theme, credited the nganga with being "a soothsayer, a prophet, a doctor of herbal medicines, a high priest, a philosopher and expounder of religion" — as well as "a brilliant medium, an expert conjuror, a sleight of hand artist" — and beyond all that, "an expertly astute businessman and a superb showman."

It was justifiable of Kaigh to credit the nganga with the brilliance of a spirit medium in light of the occurrences of a particular evening. On that night Kaigh attended a ceremony in a native village where Lokanzi propitiated the spirit of the local chieftain who had been murdered a few days before. While the villagers imbibed a native brew to the beat of native drums, Lokanzi kindled a fire in front of the dead chief's empty throne. He sprinkled the flames amply with a powdered "medicine" that gave off a pungent smoke that Kaigh described as having "a slightly stupefying effect; after smelling it, one felt a little drunk and light-headed."

That might have accounted in part for what followed. Lokanzi howled wildly, then went into a frenzied dance, while the drums beat a fierce rhythm which ended abruptly as the nganga collapsed in a deathlike trance. Moments later, a great shout rose from the onlookers, for there in the throne was the figure of the dead chief!

As Lokanzi roused from his trance, the chief talked to him;

then addressed the villagers, naming his successor and telling them who killed him. His mission accomplished, the chief rose, turned about and strode into the light of the full moon, his figure dwindling in its glow until he was gone. The murderer was later found dead, but without a mark on his body, apparently the victim of his own guilt or fear.

Exactly what happened that night is anybody's guess. It could have been an illusion created by the heavy brew and the soporific smoke; or possibly it was a case of mass hypnotism, aided by the throbbing drum beats. It might even have been a masquerade arranged by Lokanzi, or a combination of the factors mentioned; and of course, there are many people willing to believe that the witch doctor actually did materialize the spirit of the departed chief.

The term "fetish" is frequently used in connection with African witchcraft to denote an object which is "possessed" by a spiritual being. It is of European origin, however, and was originally applied to ornamental amulets worn by African natives to ward off evil, or talismans which were supposed to bring good luck. Thus the fetish may range in size from an animal's tooth to a fetish house, where a witch doctor keeps his gear and goes to consult the spirits.

Juju has a similar significance, but is more strictly a type of charm, used in connection with the witch doctor's "medicine" and can work for good or harm as required. There is some uncertainty regarding the origin of the term; some authorities claim that it comes from a native expression *grou-grou* and others believe that it is simply the French word *joujou*, meaning a plaything, because *joujoux* were often in the shape of dolls, which Europeans on the West Coast of Africa mistook for toys, never guessing what evil lurked in the hearts of those innocent looking puppets.

Some witch doctors go to the opposite extreme, making a juju that is appropriately grisly, and therefore not only impressive to the viewers, but inspirational for the operator himself. One Nigerian nganga cooked up a dandy, consisting of eight human skulls, placed jaw to jaw, all gazing upward, their foreheads bulging outward. Set upright in the center of the hollow octagon was a finely carved wooden hand, probably made by a witch doctor who believed himself a "powerful man" and who had crooned a murderous chant of hate, all during the process. Also jutting from the center of the surrounding jawbones were two simple but significant objects — a skewer and a knife. They gave the spirit killer a choice of weapons, so to speak; and also extending upright, were four human thigh bones, a good old standby of the witch doctors in every time and clime. You point one of those at anybody and he is doomed; so too with this superb Nigerian juju, the carved hand, which could do the pointing as well as the killing.

Probably each skull belonged to some good departed juju worker or somebody so vengeful in nature that the central helping hand could plug in from skull to bone, in switchboard fashion and even have two or three jobs under way at once. But when this particular juju was confiscated, only one intended murder could be charged against the owner. Tucked under one of the skulls were some torn fragments of government documents, filched from the files of an official whom the owner of the juju evidently hoped to kill.

An example of how such juju operates and the result it gains, comes from a district where a villager secretly resolved to dispose of a rival through witchcraft. The villager talked warily to a friend who was supposed to be a member of a local hyena clan, intimating that he could use their services. He was told to go to a hill outside the village, taking along a specially cooked chicken, and give a hyena call.

The villager did as he was told and in answer to his howl, lights appeared below, revealing dancers whose actions so resembled animals that at times they seemed half-human, half-hyena. One of the "hyena men" approached the awed villager and calmly ate the chicken while asking him what he wanted. The villager told him, and was in turn instructed to gather dust from his rival's footprints, charcoal from his fire, hair from his head, parings from his nails and to bring them to the next meeting, along with a full grown black goat.

On the night the villager returned with the required articles he was again met by the juju man of the hyena clan, who sprinkled the goat with powdered "medicine" and drove it off into the jungle as a sacrifice. Whether it was to be killed and eaten by wild animals or members of the hyena clan, he did not specify. The juju man then produced some straw from the hut of the villager's rival, crammed it into a hole in the ground and added the rival's personal effects that the villager had brought.

Setting fire to the lot, the juju man pointed in the direction of the intended victim's hut and chanted a command to "Kill — Kill — Kill!" as he sprinkled powdered "medicine" on the flames. When the fire died down, he extinguished it by filling the hole with dirt and marking the spot so that after the charm fulfilled its purpose, the ashes could be dug up and scattered. Without such a precaution it could continue to function, perhaps adversely, toward the jujuist or his client, or even members of the hyena clan.

The trouble was, the juju worked too well. Within three days the victim died — so suddenly and so mysteriously that his relatives suspected witchcraft. Checking persons who had been antagonistic toward him, they watched the villager and trailed him when he went to meet the jujuist and dig up the buried evidence. So both were brought to justice. Penalties for witchcraft are stringent in Africa, as court records will show; but they can be even tougher when native justice takes over. Suspected witches may be beaten to death, impaled with spears or burned alive. Sometimes a grass hut with a witch doctor inside, has burst into flames. That isn't much different from the days when they set fire to a witch's cottage in England. Always a witch's body should be burned, not only to prevent some evil spirit from animating it, which would be quite dreadful; but because a capable nganga can use the bones and ashes to make "medicine" which may prove helpful in thwarting the designs of other witches.

Among many African tribes, any death was attributed to witchcraft unless it could be proved otherwise. That was logical, considering that there was no good reason for anybody ever to die, unless killed by some animal or person; and even then, there might have been some hidden scheme behind it. So witch finders were constantly in vogue, just as in more civilized climes, their business being to "smell out" any suspects responsible for the unusual deaths. Here is an account of such a ceremony, from only a few decades back:

A big fire was built in the center of the village and the women retired to their huts, while the men formed a kneeling row, until the nganga arrived. He was preceded by two assistants wearing skirted costumes and waving torches, their eyes and foreheads smeared with white clay, giving them a ghostly appearance. As they danced and shouted, the witch doctor put in his appearance in far more fearful guise, wearing a weird mask with huge teeth and towering crown. Soon, the torch bearers waved the men to their huts; then one brought a "medicine bag" and handed it to the nganga along with a small basket decorated with shells, skin and dried blood.

From the bag, the nganga took several grisly objects which he dropped into the basket; then put on the lid. He and his helpers then began a round of the huts; one beating a drum, the other calling the names of the occupants, who came out one by one. With each, the weirdly masked witch doctor raised the lid of the basket and nodded that the man was clear. So one by one, the villagers joined the procession in ever-gathering force, until at one hut, the lid refused to come free when a man was called. That meant that the spirits controlling the fetish had gripped his soul and were holding it there. That proved that the man — or woman — was guilty of witchcraft unless he, or she, could prove otherwise. Often, accused victims were too overwhelmed to speak up in their own defense, so they became the victims of mob violence or whatever fate the witch doctor might decree. But if an accused person insisted that he was innocent, there was one sure way to tell whether he was right or wrong. That was to have him undergo an ordeal and see what resulted.

The poison test was among the best. The nganga mixed a brew of sassy bark, grimaced when he tasted it and then let the suspect have a try. Normally, such revolting stuff should sicken him; if it did, he was deemed innocent; but if his stomach retained it, he was doomed. The reason was simple enough — the poison was fighting the evil spirits within him, automatically proving that he was a witch. Usually, it worked against the suspect, since the witch doctor, rather than lose face by picking an innocent man, was apt to go lightly on the poison, so the suspect would be able to stomach the brew.

A missionary in the old Cameroon territory, which is now part of the Republic of Cameroon, was credited with challenging a witch doctor to drink his own poison brew on the chance that he, too, might be a witch. When the nganga refused, the case against the suspect was dropped. This simply proves that a witch doctor is not infallible; in fact, in some localities, a distinction is made between such practitioners as an *inyanga*, or mere "bone-thrower," and an *insangoma* or "smeller-outer."

While a nganga is supposed to use his power only for good and never for evil, it is difficult to draw a sharp line of demarcation between the two. A witch doctor, to be worthy of the name, must be acquainted with all the devices used by witches; hence there might be times when he would find it expedient to fight bad medicine with bad medicine. If a witch should send a *ngozi*, or grudge-bearing spirit, to harm a witch doctor's client, the quickest remedy might be to send another *ngozi* after the offending witch. The same would apply to a type of witchcraft sometimes called *izulu*, in which natural elements, particularly lightning, are used to strike a victim.

The incongruous angle is that in cases where a witch doctor cooks up some imaginary case or type of witchcraft, where nobody is really involved, any counteracting measure of his own would mean that he alone was practicing witchcraft. But if you add nothing to nothing, you still have nothing, so it is hard to tell where the vicious circle begins or ends.

African witchcraft supplies a surprising parallel to European witch lore, most notably in the way that witches flit about at night. Where English witches relied on broomsticks, their African counterparts preferred various animals, chiefly the hyena, but quite frequently the ant-bear, or aardvark, a piglike creature that measures as much as six feet. It goes scouting about for ants, as its name implies, and therefore has nocturnal habits.

That made it easy for witches to coax such a creature from its favorite ant-hill and commandeer it for a rapid ride through the void. Another unusual animal, the ant-wolf, is somewhat of a cross between the hyena and the aardvark, making the link all the stronger. Hence, in parts of Africa, if somebody happens to kill an ant-bear, it may prove to be the familiar of some witch, who having lost her favorite steed, promptly puts a whammy on the unsuspecting perpetrator. Unfortunately, he doesn't realize how he sinned until he consults a witch doctor and obtains a full diagnosis of his problem.

Other factors figure in African witchcraft, such as the rhythmic drum beats that throb through the jungle darkness, strumming unspoken messages for all to hear. To learn what evil really lurks in the hearts of men, you have only to study cases of miscreants who are literally hounded to their deserved doom by the monotonous thrum-thrum of the jungle drums.

The drum was regarded as having a life of its own by such tribes as the Batangas, who did more than merely cover a big drum with a fresh cowskin; they let the animal's blood flow into the drum. For good measure, they occasionally beheaded a man and added his blood, too. That meant that whenever the drum was beaten, their king would get a new extension of life from the spirit of the victim.

Where witchcraft was somewhat "touch and go" with other tribes, the Ashanti located in what is now Ghana, counted on it to win battles. Ashanti witches worked in league with an all-powerful demon named Sasabonsam, who took the shape of a hairy monster with long legs and feet that pointed in two directions. The Ashanti also used women witch finders, who wore white robes and smeared their faces with white clay. Then, in honor of a very special fetish, they did a shuffling, stooping dance to the beat of a huge drum. In fact, fetishism played such an important role in the lives of the Ashanti that their king was compelled to have 3,333 wives. On one occasion, he and his cohorts defeated and killed a British governor, whose skull was made into a royal drinking mug, which was something of a fetish in itself.

A half century later, the Ashanti lost a bitter war in which the king's palace in Kumasi was blown up and a great spirit house located in a sacred grove, was burned. That was in 1874; in 1896, another war culminated in the destruction of a new palace and more fetish buildings. The Ashanti territory was annexed by the Gold Coast colony five years later; and is now part of the new and independent Republic of Ghana. Today, Kumasi is a thriving commercial city and in its colorful market place, customers from all over Ghana can buy anything from canned goods to ready-made fetishes. But witchcraft is not only still alive in Africa, it has traveled far from there and flourishes strongly in other parts of the world as a final survey will show.

15
Voodoo and Modern Devil Worship

To appreciate witchcraft as it stands today, it must be considered not only in terms of its origins, but its survival, expansion, extension, and above all, whatever new vitality it has gained. The final point is most important, because witchcraft, like everything else in our complex world, must strike a popular tempo and fill some modern need to win itself support. To say that witchcraft has done just that is putting it mildly indeed.

The primitive witchcraft of the Australian bushmen, which can still be found in a pristine state today, has been directly linked to the ultra-modern subject of ESP or extra sensory perception; and the same applies to many beliefs, rituals and superstitions found in Malaysia, India, China, Mongolia, and even the hinterlands of

Europe and America. All this, however, is to be expected; of greater interest is the fact that such things have taken new root and found new growth in surroundings even more lush than those from whence they originated. That brings up a prime example of the witchcraft of today — voodoo.

According to good authorities, witchcraft in the West Indies is of two distinct patterns — *obeah*, or *obi*, a direct outgrowth, indeed almost a transplant, of Ashanti beliefs. It is found in various islands, most notably Jamaica, because many members of the Ashanti and related tribes were brought there as slaves. They, in turn, brought their witchcraft with them and gradually obeah men emerged, whose powers resembled that of their Ashanti counterparts.

Some critics of obeah claim that it is truly diabolical and therefore all bad; but others refuse to go along with that opinion. They point out that obeah, as a power to work evil, is partly balanced *myalism*, or a power to work good; and that the same practitioner can apply himself to both, though he is more apt to specialize in one or the other.

A mean trick of the obeah man is to steal away a person's shadow, or at least the spirit that supposedly dwells therein, and to spellbind or "nail" it to the great silk-cotton tree, the chosen residence of that great evil spirit Sasabonsam, the same malignant entity so dreaded by the Ashanti. Thus deprived of his shadow, the owner is sure to pine away and die, if for no reason other than the fact that he and everybody else believe that he will do so.

But if a myal man can pick out the right tree and conduct the correct ritual, he can loosen the enthralled shadow and catch it departing from the tree. He may need the help of assistants to make sure of returning it to its shadowless owner, and back in the 1890's, the going price for such a job was six dollars. No recent quotations are available but they would naturally run much higher.

Many more intriguing facets of obeah could be discussed in detail, but they would simply reiterate much of what has already been related regarding African witchcraft. In contrast, voodoo, while also of African origin, has spread its roots so far and wide, and has had such intriguing phases of development, that it has had far more impact on the world at large. In Haiti, Africans of many unrelated tribes and cultures were brought together and, through sheer necessity, began to share one another's languages and beliefs. Thus they developed remarkable rites that are distinctive in themselves, yet with many variations of their own.

All rites begin with a supplication to Papa Legba, gate-keeper of the voodoo Valhalla, to "open the way" for worshipers to appeal to other members of the pantheon. The major gods may come from almost any part of Africa, but their ranks have been so amplified by all grades of divinities and local spirits, that it would take dozens of pages merely to list them in small print. These include the souls of many departed *hungans* and *mambos*, who served as priests and priestesses, respectively, at voodoo rites. So, even in compiling a list, it might be incomplete by the time you reached Zaka, the popular god who patronizes farmers and their crops, since new deities might have cropped up in the meantime.

Hence, a survey of voodoo, from the standpoint of witchcraft, must necessarily be confined to the methods used and the results gained. Perhaps the commonest way to begin is with the old reliable "devil doll," which has figured so regularly in witchcraft everywhere, but seems to be unusually popular and potent in Haiti. A striking case was that of a U.S. Marine captain who became an officer in the Haitian gendarmerie. One day during inspection he found a braided horsehair effigy hanging from his saddle. How and when it was placed there, he didn't know, but he disregarded the *wanga*, as the thing was called, and simply hung it in his hut as a souvenir. A few days later, that saddle unexplainably came loose as he was mounting his horse and he was nearly killed in the runaway that followed.

A more powerful procedure is for a hungan to conjure up an image of a person in a pail of water; then stab it with a knife. If the water turns red like blood, the victim will die. This ritual has apparently been witnessed on many occasions, but it raises a question as to where witchcraft leaves off and trickery takes over.

Granting that even a reliable witness might imagine he saw an image in the water — even mistaking the reflection of his own face for someone else's — it might still be impossible to convince him that water turned blood red unless it did.

There, the juice of some tropical plant, applied to the knife blade, might supply the crimson dye that would add reality to illusion, for those who know their voodoo are often skilled herbalists as well, and there could well be occasions when death by some secret poison has been timed to an appropriate ritual.

But these are mere trifles compared to other voodoo tales that run the gamut from the bizarre to the macabre. These include weird sacrifices to Damballah, the Serpent God; ritualistic dances held in jungle clearings, driving the participants to mad fury by the beat of tom-toms; the hand of a dead hungan rising to point out his young successor, so he can recall his own departed spirit and transplant it with all its wisdom in the mind and body of someone who can use it well.

Wandering ghosts of various types thrive in the tropical atmosphere of the West Indies. In obeah, some of the most malevolent are termed "duppies" or "jumbies" and voodoo has its counterparts. Vampires take on the shape of great birds that might snatch anyone on a dark night, and not many years ago, there was talk of an automobile called a "tiger car" that prowled the streets of Port-au-Prince, the Haitian capital, making off with unsuspecting victims.

Most startling of all are the "zombies" or walking dead, who are presumably the products of highly virulent witchcraft, which is used to draw a spirit from a human being, causing the person to die. His body can then be animated through powers known only to voodoo, so that it becomes a mere machine, serving only its voodoo master. Tales are told of troops of zombies being marched down from the hills and signed up as workers cutting sugar cane by a clever operator who collects their wages for himself.

They require little upkeep, except scant portions of tasteless food — enough to keep them going mechanically; but care must be taken not to feed them certain substances, especially salt. It can revive their sense of taste, and with it, a homing instinct that enables them to march right back to their graves and burrow themselves beyond any further voodoo influence. Also, there is always the chance that zombies may be seen and recognized by friends who frequently reclaim them and take physical vengeance on the voodoo man.

The zombie legend provides some definite clues regarding the physical factors involved in voodoo. Hypnotism unquestionably plays a major part in all voodoo rituals, starting with the commanding presence of the hungan or the mambo, gaining force from the incessant drum beats and reaching its zenith in the contagious effect of the dance, plus the crackle and blaze of voodoo fires. Often, persons recalling the fantastic things they witnessed are forced to agree that they were under some hypnotic influence.

Drugs are another explanation. Marijuana, and other hallucinatory products are sometimes used; and there are subtle poisons of tropical origin, unquestionably known to specialists in voodoo. Certain mysterious ailments, such as the African sleeping sickness, often induce a coma-like state that could give rise to a zombie rumor. All this accounts for the popularity of voodoo charms as preventive measures.

Voodoo has traveled far from Haiti, a reason why it has become such a significant factor in the witchcraft of today, as we shall see.

One of the earliest points of contact for voodoo in the United States was New Orleans, way back when Haiti and Louisiana were both French colonies. Powders, potions, perfumes for all purposes are now available almost anywhere. So, too, are voodoo dolls — complete with pins. While their appeal is chiefly to ignorant purchasers, the intelligentsia fall for such things, too.

In the early part of the twentieth century, "civilized" people, rather than take up voodoo, which they passed off as pure nonsense and jungle superstition, turned to its predecessor — Satanism. Their leader was a debonair disciple of the Devil, named Aleister Crowley, who claimed to be the Beast with the Number 666 mentioned in the Book of Revelation.

Aleister Crowley had attained a peak as a Satanist early in 1914, according to American "tramp poet" Harry Kemp, who was living in London at that time. Through an artist friend, Kemp learned of the mystical — and almost mythical — leader of a fantastic cult, who conducted diabolical ceremonies as its "high priest" in some obscure, buried retreat. But Kemp was utterly unable to meet the sinister master or learn any more about the strange devil cult, until one night when he and the artist were dining in the Cafe Royal. Suddenly the artist pointed out a slightly balding middle-aged man, with a curious lock of hair extending down his forehead.

"There!" the artist confided in a breathless undertone. "There is the high priest of the weird cult I told you about!"

Staring toward the corner table where the strange man sat, Kemp met the gaze of sharp, dark eyes; small and piercing, like gimlets. Lowering his own gaze, Kemp noted that the man's plump and very whitish fingers were covered with ornate rings. Kemp pressed the artist for an introduction then and there, though his friend undertoned a warning that he might be sorry if he mixed with even the fringes of what the artist now pronounced to be a "damnable" cult. But Kent persisted, so the artist caught the strange man's eye, received a nod, and conducted Kemp to the corner table, where soon the three were happily sipping absinthe, the most potent drink available.

Such was Kemp's meeting with Aleister Crowley, the remarkable man whom William Somerset Maugham had already immortalized under the name of "Oliver Haddo" in an early novel titled *The Magician*. Kemp found the devil master cordial and engaging, with the result that he was invited to call at Crowley's studio the next week. Kemp went and his description of the place was graphic indeed. He was admitted by a girl clad in a black robe and literally found himself enveloped in a purple cloud created by the smoke of exotic incense streaming from surrounding burners.

Black curtains served as dividers to form three rooms. The first was walled with rows of bookcases containing black leather-bound books, bearing silver cabalistic signs, for titles. The second room was fitted with divans and floor cushions where visitors could loll while they awaited developments. The third room had a black altar topped by a golden circle with a lifelike emblem of a golden serpent zigzagging across it. Above was a canopy, while the floor below bore cabalistic signs.

Kemp was shown all this by Crowley himself and he found that the black-bound books represented a vast collection of rare volumes on all forms of mythology, mysticism and witchcraft — black and white. But it was not until three months later that he won the high priest's confidence sufficiently to be invited to attend a meeting of the Satanic cult — a meeting which Kemp branded as a "Black Mass."

The worshipers who thronged the place all appeared to be of high social status, though each wore a black domino mask to hide his or her identity. The only light in the weird room flickered from a seven-branch candlestick, which was suddenly extinguished. From the Stygian blackness came the solemn voice of Aleister Crowley, the mighty Satanist himself, reciting the cult's creed:

> *There is no good. Evil itself is good. Blessed be the principle of evil. All hail, Prince of the World, to whom even God Himself has given dominion.*

Amid a bleating response, a ghostly light pervaded the room, and through a haze of sickening incense, Kemp saw a huge crystal globe emerge from the floor, giving off clouds of white smoke that materialized into the shapes of midget dancing demons who cavorted fantastically to the weird wail of a distant flute and the throb of unseen drums. One woman screamed and tore away her mask, revealing a handsome but thoroughly panic-stricken face. She was led out through the curtains while the rites continued, uninterrupted.

As the demons vanished, the candles ignited again and Kemp saw Crowley, attired in his Satanic robes, step forward to the altar, where he picked up an oddly shaped knife. Raising his chant to a high piercing pitch, he ripped open the front of his robe and stabbed himself repeatedly in the breast. As his disciples pressed eagerly forward and knelt before him, he marked their foreheads with strange cabalistic symbols drawn with his own oozing blood.

From then on, according to Kemp, the worshipers went berserk, some tearing off their clothes as they danced about, raising their voices in obscene, blasphemous chants. In the midst of the hideous orgy, Kemp escaped to the street and made his way back to his digs in the light of early dawn. He arrived there safely enough, for all this had happened, not in some underworld section of London, but in a house set in a garden on Fulham Road, in the highly respectable suburb of Kensington.

It took the tramp poet a long while to get over his fantastic experience. When he related the events to his artist friend, the latter agreed that he, too, had been shaken after attending one of Crowley's Satanic ceremonies. As the artist put it, "You have come into contact with the powers of darkness and they do not want to let you go." So Kemp packed up and headed home to America, where he salved his conscience by revealing the secrets of the Satanists, putting it all into a feature story under his own byline.

That happened just before the outbreak of World War I. Within a few months, Crowley, too, returned to the States as things in Europe were in such a hellish state that even a Satanist couldn't stand it there. Crowley promptly issued a denial of Kemp's account, which the newspaper printed in rebuttal. In it, Crowley was quoted as saying that "Kemp honestly believes he was present at the things he describes, but he wasn't. I merely made him dream a scene of black magic and he thought it was actually happening and that I was participating. He dreamed it himself."

Crowley went on to describe more beneficent rites in which he admitted participating, such as evoking the spirit of Mars in the form of hidden occult forces, so the world might know what lay in store for it. Symbolically, Crowley had worn a blood-red robe, while his two associate students of the occult, a high-ranking

British naval officer and a famous violinist, wore robes of white and gold. That incident, Crowley claimed, had taken place four years before, and the invoked spirit, which Crowley described as "sexless and oxlike" had materialized amid clouds of incense with its "hideous human features suffused with blood," while it hoarsely prophesied that Europe was on the verge of a destructive great war.

Crowley spent the war years in America, establishing branches of his London cult. Occasionally, he retreated to an island eighty miles up the Hudson River, near Kingston, New York, to engage in deep contemplation. There, for the benefit of passengers on river steamers, he painted a statement in huge red letters:

*DO WHAT THOU WILT
SHALL BE
THE WHOLE OF THE LAW*

That summed Crowley's creed, which found its widest acceptance in Manhattan's Greenwich Village, a rendezvous for people who were willing to try anything, not just once, but often. There, in his "Temple of Darkness," Beast 666 taught his disciples that the world was peopled by witches, demons and devils, dating from the satyrs of Greek mythology and their kindred spirit, the god Pan. Soon, new tales of his Satanic rites were confirming the spicy reports that Kemp had made. In the wake of these scandals that were beginning to undermine his cult, the Beast decided to decamp for a fresher field.

Crowley chose Cefalu, in Sicily, where he set up a sex cult called the Abbey of Thelema, which attracted some of his most rabid — and wealthiest — followers to date. But the sudden death of a young Englishman under somewhat unexplainable circumstances forced Crowley to leave Italy for France. However, his stay there was also short-lived, and he was soon ordered out of France when word leaked out that he was planning Satanic rites in Paris. All this made sensational headlines in the pulp London weeklies where Crowley was branded as "The King of Depravity," "A Human Beast," "A Cannibal at Large," and the "Wickedest Man in the World."

Shortly after Crowley's escape from France, a book appeared, giving inside stories of the Order of the Temple of the Orient — O.T.O. — Crowley's witchcraft cult of his Greenwich Village days. The book claimed that he had utilized a rare South American drug to make his clients see fantastic colors and impossible creatures. The book also listed the contents of A.C.'s favorite cocktail, the Kubla Khan Number Two, which consisted of unspecified amounts of gin and vermouth, plus lesser quantities from two other bottles, one being labeled "Poison." The informant found out later that the "poison" bottle contained laudanum, a tincture of opium. When Crowley sued the author for libel, his case was thrown out of court by an English judge, who classed as "blasphemous" some of Crowley's ritualistic chants that were quoted in the book.

All this simply roused new interest in devil cults and other forms of witchcraft, which sprouted in ever-increasing numbers, particularly in England. Aleister Crowley lived until 1954 and when he died in Brighton, there was a grand turnout of members of mystic cults at his funeral. Needless to say, it was celebrated in true pagan style. Scotland Yard was particularly interested in this very special funeral because it was steadily stepping up its investigations of secret organizations of the Satanic type that Crowley sponsored.

According to police reports, these groups form a veritable web that can enmesh unsuspecting victims in an ever-increasing tangle. The first step may be mere attendance at a lecture on some phase of witchcraft, where newcomers are approached and asked if they would like to witness a meeting or ritual of the type discussed. Similarly, an obscure bookstore handling volumes on metaphysical subjects can be the "front" for secret backroom meeting places. So-called "spirit séances" are also stepping stones to devil worship, as materialization of ghostly forms is their ultimate objective.

Small, third-rate hotels were also watched by Scotland Yard, particularly those with rooms so poorly furnished that it was a wonder why anybody would stay in them — although nobody really did. Instead, guests were conducted to the cellar, then through a secret door that was probably an old fireplace, into an adjacent basement where a closet was unlocked, with all the mystery of Bluebeard's castle, to reveal a circular staircase leading up to a Satanic Temple. After all that mumbo jumbo, a neophyte would be definitely conditioned for anything — from the worship of a hideous tropical idol to the celebration of a Black Mass.

In contrast to all this, there has been a concerted effort to revive witchcraft on a benign scale, with the claim that it is the "old religion," dating back even before the Druids. The chief advocate of this practice was a well-traveled Englishman, Dr. Gerald Gardner, who had studied primitive customs throughout the world and regarded many of them as offshoots of the "old religion" mixed with other beliefs. While Aleister Crowley was still finding himself unwelcome and unwanted in havens where he hoped to propagate his Satanic ceremonies, Gerald Gardner was serenely establishing himself on the Isle of Man, in the Irish Sea, equidistant from England, Scotland and Ireland.

The Isle of Man was an ideal site for Gardner and his followers because it was steeped in lore of fairy-folk and witchcraft. It was also the cross-roads for many invading races and, even today, it has the status of a kingdom in its own right, with its government founded on the old Norse parliament. Hence the attitude toward witchcraft was different than in England, where the laws forbidding it were not repealed until as late as 1951. But the Isle of Man offered another attraction for a lover of the primitive like Dr. Gardner; thanks to its equable, sunny climate and its liberal laws, a nudist colony was thriving there, offering an opportunity to combine two popular cults.

Dr. Gardner added a new twist to an old distinction between "black" and "white" witchcraft, which supposedly represented the bad and good sides of the coin. He linked horrible deeds for which witches had so often been condemned, with diabolical rites in which evil spirits were invoked. That was the reason why a circle was drawn around the invokers — to keep the forces of evil from storming in and overwhelming their conjure-uppers.

Now, according to Dr. Gardner, good witches needed a surrounding circle to contain the power which they personally generated or exuded, until they were ready to launch it forth into the void as a full-fledged psychic power. By that same sound logic, Dr. G. decided that clothing would cramp the process. In order to charge the circle properly, nudism was the only answer. Hence neophytes should be introduced to the sacred circle wearing only a blindfold; and when divested of even that, they would find that the other members of the coven were also in the altogether, ready to participate in the initiation.

What a surprise! What an initiation! What fun! Anyway, that's how it was, how it is, and probably will be, regardless of how it should be. Based upon such a premise, witch cults have been on the increase in England ever since, until at last report there were an estimated 6,000 witches — masculine, feminine and possibly neuter — operating in England alone. Reports throughout Europe are almost as encouraging and, even in America, scattered returns show that witchcraft is on the rise.

Good, or white witches limit themselves to groups of thirteen to a coven, usually six men and six women, with a high priest or priestess presiding over them. According to some authorities, thirteen has always been the magic number for a coven and records of certain witchcraft trials show that just that number of suspects were involved. Where there were less, it could have meant that the witchfinders simply hadn't caught up with the rest, or that the coven was short-handed. Where there were more than thirteen, it indicated that members of two or more covens were involved. At the roundup of witches charged with raising a storm to wreck the ship that was bringing King James of Scotland home from Denmark, thirty-nine suspects were involved, which meant that three covens were working on the job.

Yet that didn't prove that storm-raising witches were all bad. It just depended on who was to be wrecked and why. After the Spanish Armada was defeated by the English fleet, its ships were scattered and many wrecked by a totally unexpected storm that could have been the wish of English witches. When Napoleon was planning a sea invasion of England, storms helped to ruin his hopes. That bit of history repeated itself on a still greater scale when Hitler planned a similar invasion during World War II, and, in that case, English witches openly took credit for raising the devastating storms that repeatedly thwarted the Nazis from making their attempt.

Still, witches can't be all good, either. In extolling the rites used by the benign English witches, Dr. Gardner added a distinctly dubious note when he stated: "The only man I can think of who could have invented the rites was the late Aleister Crowley ... There are indeed certain expressions and certain words used which smack of Crowley; possibly he borrowed things from the cult writings, or more likely someone may have borrowed expressions from him." — a good point to remember before joining a coven of modern witches in an innocent frolic. It may be just another way of giving the Devil his due.

16
Witchcraft Today ... and Tomorrow

Judged by existing trends, and with a concerted effort on the part of the practitioners, witchcraft in the future may zoom to proportions that could become alarming. However, the field is still in such a state of flux that it is impossible to compile a reliable Who's Who in Witchcraft; in fact, it is difficult even to determine Which's Witch. Apparently, all you have to say is, "I am a witch!" and you are one, as measured by your own yardstick.

Very little formal education is needed; perhaps the less, the better. One bouncy British witch admits to only three years of orthodox schooling, yet poses as the absolute authority on witchcraft, past, present and future. The accumulation of such erudition without study or research would be incongruous, except in witchcraft, which is incongruous in itself. Witches don't have to read books to absorb the knowledge contained therein; they just sleep on them. Or they can use a Ouija Board to tune in on unseen entities that will provide them with first-hand facts that never were recorded.

There has been so much talk of modern witches in rural England that anyone might suppose that the woods are full of them. But such is far from so. In the New Forest, long the traditional haunt of English witches, there were at recent report, only four active covens in an area larger than the entire District of Columbia. Yet this has been cited as proof that the witch cult has continued its uninterrupted course since antiquity, despite the fact that the "old religion" went out with the Druids around A.D. 67, while the New Forest was established as such by William the Conqueror, ten years after his victory at Hastings in 1066. That gap of a thousand years is a bit too big for even witchery to charm away.

Some members of rural covens can trace their ancestry back to victims of witchcraft persecutions; but those took place long after the Norman Conquest; and besides, most of the victims were falsely accused and therefore weren't witches at all. So any lore they handed down through successive generations can be classed as assorted superstitions, rather than the survival of ancient rituals. Since gypsies have long roamed the English countryside, their customs and curses have also roused the interest of today's self-styled witches; but since historians claim that the gypsies did not arrive in England until about 1500, linking them with the "old religion" would be ridiculous indeed, unless the gypsies happened to be the Druids coming back to Britain after long wanderings elsewhere; a better theory, perhaps, than some that have been seriously propounded.

Coming to London, the scene changes. While the rustic witches devote time to gathering herbs, tickling trout and furthering fertility festivals, like the Great Sabbats, their city cousins gather at neighborhood pubs and repair to nearby apartments to hold regular meetings, or esbats, where new candidates are initiated into the craft. This constantly increases the size of the covens, enabling them to subdivide like unicellular creatures and spread microscopically through the teeming life of the city, attracting new recruits until they reach the ultimate thirteen and are ready for another fission.

This results in loosely associated groups, all following a similar ritual and purpose. One acknowledged "King of the Witches" is credited with more than a hundred covens under his paternal tutelage. To prove how innocuous their ceremonies could be, he invited a camera crew to make a documentary film of a full-fledged initiation. A chalk circle nine feet in diameter was drawn on the carpeted floor of the snug meeting room, leaving the camera crew outside, though there was barely room for them. There was also barely room within the circle for what transpired there. The coven became "skyclad" by divesting themselves of all raiment and accoutrements, other than such ornaments as bracelets, chains and lockets, which were necessarily of silver, the metal symbolic of the moon.

The ritual, too, was "symbolic" insofar as its physical phases were concerned. After a customary chant, the witches went into a serpentine dance that took skilled footing to avoid winding up in a tangle like a juvenile parlor game. Following that, the initiate was introduced, threatened with a sword point, flicked lightly with a lash, as preludes to further and more sensual symbolism, based upon "Aradia," or the so-called "Gospel of the Witches." But such rituals, however platonic or well-intentioned they may be, far transcend the proprieties allowable with a television documentary.

That in itself is proof that much more could transpire at an esbat than meets the camera's eye; and no one is more aware of that than those long schooled in witchcraft. Once a new coven is launched, it becomes hard indeed to control it; and only too often some renegade group decides to switch from white witchcraft to black magic. Far from being difficult, that is sometimes too easy. Often, a person with a natural flare for witchcraft can sense the presence of evil entities along with good and must therefore cultivate the practice of banishing the bad by summoning the good.

All that can be reversed by drawing the circle the wrong way to keep spirits out instead of in. The good will stay away, but the bad throng about, hoping to break through the circle. By judicious use of cabalistic and necromantic rites, such powers can be bound and commanded to do the evoker's bidding. Things might go badly indeed with a camera crew attempting to film such a ritual. Left outside the circle, they would become targets of the frustrated evil entities who were unable to get at those within, and would be badly battered along with their equipment.

From this, it is painfully plain that when such forces are sent on their way at the evoker's order, trouble is due for anyone named as their victim. When word of such renegade activities gets back to the parent coven, its duty is obvious. In keeping with the "do good" policy that is the watchword of modern witchcraft, they cannot fight evil with evil. So they create a new cone of power at the next esbat and launch it like a miniature tornado in the direction of the offender, hoping to score a direct hit. By the old law that evil is its own undoing, the power of good turns those baleful influences back on the renegade who sponsored them, so that he suffers the harm he sought to inflict upon unsuspecting victims.

That still leaves a question unanswered; namely, why any coven, whatever its attitude, should set itself up as judge of right or wrong. As do-gooders, witches are apt to overdo things. Suppose a coven decides to further a girl's romance by concentrating their massed power on a boyfriend who has been ignoring her. If their efforts fail to click, the next step is to provide the lovelorn damsel with a love potion to bring him around; and if a rival for his affections should enter the scene, something still more potent might be recommended. Witchery has its own pharmacopeia, as every herb gatherer knows, and members of city covens know where to obtain the necessary powders that take over when powers fail.

A charming lack of consistency permeates the British witchcraft scene. One British witch who came to America to "sell" the craft in a big way, suddenly decided that astrology was her "first love" as taught to her by her old grandmother. Why her old grandmother would have been looking up at the stars while digging herbs, is rather puzzling in itself. A likelier explanation is that when the visiting witch observed the grip that astrology had already gained on the American public, she decided to tie it in with witchcraft, as an added selling point.

Other occult subjects have also been teamed with witchcraft. Some witches delve deeply into the mysteries of the tarots, or fortune telling cards, even dealing the pack all the way around the circle during an esbat, to intensify the influences drawn therein. Others use crystal gazing as a guide toward the formation of a coven, confident that faces seen in the crystal ball will be those of future members, who will be recognized in due course. Tea-leaf reading and palmistry are also highly favored, being akin to gypsy witchery. Yet there are some who take the opposite attitude, avoiding anything that savors of "fortune telling," presumably on the theory that the purpose of witchcraft is to shape the future, rather than be swayed by it.

One thing on which many witches are thoroughly in accord is the "Book of Shadows," which is regarded as a "must" for those who hope to rise high in the craft. Basically, it sets forth the Law of the Wicca, or the "wise folk," the term that witches have long applied to themselves; and to it may be added whatever personalized data seems sufficiently important. One of a graduate witch's first assignments is to copy or write his own "Book of Shadows" so that if he is caught with it, it will appear to be unique and therefore cannot involve others of the craft. Here, however, new discrepancies present themselves.

The "Book of Shadows" treats witchcraft as though it were very ancient, thereby bearing out its claim as the "old religion." But the book itself is obviously of medieval origin, as it is filled with advice on how to avoid persecution and mislead inquisitors, showing that it could hardly have been written until witch hunts were gathering real momentum. But it is doubtful that it was written even then, for two good reasons: First, the witches of that period were generally too illiterate even to read the rules, let alone write them; while second, and more important, the admonitions themselves were *prima facie* evidence that witchcraft was operating on a large scale in the form of covens, which could have been rounded up quite handily. Hence possession of such a book would not have been worth the risk, even though some member of the coven was supposed to destroy any such book immediately after the owner's death, unless the owner had already done so.

It is highly possible that the "Book of Shadows" made its first appearance long after witchcraft persecutions ceased and new generations of the craft were literate enough to write down sayings that had been passed along by word of mouth; and also felt safe enough to do so. There are skeptics, however, who feel that the "Book of Shadows" is a strictly modern concoction designed for the instruction of present-day covens, but given old-time nomenclature to make it seem traditional. The same applies to the phrase, "Blessed be," which today's witches use in greeting one another, as well as such chants as "Eko, Eko, Azarak; Eko, Eko, Aradia," which are used to raise the "cone of power," but are of Italian origin rather than British.

No matter how synthetic British witchcraft may have become, the mere weight of tradition has given it status and the success of its covens has done much to spread interest in other lands. Many witches have been welcomed by European covens, giving the craft an international status. But that has produced complications, as one English coven learned when approached by a delegation from India, who wanted them to officiate at the rededication of a long neglected temple. The Hindus turned out to be worshipers of Kali, the goddess of destruction and death; and when they casually announced that the ceremony would feature a human sacrifice, they were astonished that the English witches refused to have a part in it.

Nor was their surprise unjustified. The visitors had evidently been impressed by the claim that the current revival of witchcraft in Britain was a direct link to the "old religion" and therefore to the Druids, whose rites had been suppressed because they included human sacrifice. There are also certain similarities between the traditional worship of Diana and that of Kali. Just as Diana has her opposite in Hecate, so does Kali have "another self" in Devi. The sacrifice of small animals, such as dogs and cats, as well as chickens, was definitely charged to British witches when their persecution was at its height; and today, in Calcutta, there are regularly scheduled sacrifices of goats and calves, at Kalighat, a temple erected about the year 1809 on a site sacred to Kali.

As an added touch, it might be noted that at that time a secret society of stranglers known as the "Thugs" was rampant in India. Its members traveled in bands, killing and robbing unsuspecting victims, all in honor of Kali. The thugs operated in response to omens, exchanged greetings in a jargon of their own as a means of identifying one another and piously poured a portion of their loot into coffers reserved for Kali. Their form of human sacrifice, known as "Thuggee," was all but obliterated during the period of British rule in India, chiefly between 1828 and 1835, so in a sense, they suffered at the hands of the same Establishment that had persecuted the English witches several centuries earlier. With the formation of the Republic of India in 1949 and the repeal of the British Witchcraft Laws in 1953, it would seem that the old religions of Kali and Diana should have found something in common, but they didn't. Even when the Hindu delegation promised to provide victims who would not only be willing, but would deem it an honor to be sacrificed on Kali's altar, the straight-laced English witches refused to go along.

In America, witchcraft has taken a trend quite different from that of the cozy covens found in England. According to one estimate, there were some 400 covens in the United States, which would account for from 4,000 to 5,000 witches, not too far short of the British total of 6,000. However, considering that most of the island of Great Britain could be squeezed into the state of Idaho, which it somewhat resembles in shape, the American covens must obviously be scattered far and wide.

Having little in common with their English counterparts, except through hearsay, the American covens tend to be individualistic and self-sufficient to such degree that would-be witches are continually complaining that they can't find a coven to join and don't know how to start one of their own. So the estimate of 400 may itself be sheer guesswork. Yet one modern warlock who lives in Massachusetts insists that there are more than a hundred covens in New England alone. That is logical, considering that New England was the traditional home of American witchcraft, back when matters were equally hot in Old England. But like other American covens, those of New England have a way of meeting secretly, much like the early college fraternities and sororities.

In contrast to the close-knit coven system, America has inherited numerous forms of witchcraft from various ethnic groups that brought their traditions with them and were allowed to keep them unmolested, except in rare instances. That could partially account for the secretive factor; but there is another element, too. Intermingling of races and nationalities, beginning from the first contacts of European settlers with the native Indians, have resulted in a curious and remarkable intermingling of all phases of witchery. This was noted by a folklore foundation, some thirty years ago, with the result that an exhaustive survey was taken in a single county in the state of Illinois, where the foundation workers came up with more than 10,000 superstitions and bygone beliefs, all relevant to witchcraft and all accepted today.

From this it is obvious that witchcraft in America tends to develop spontaneously, rather than through the stylized formalities of the English covens, or the intense and highly emotional fervor encountered in many other lands. Taken from that standpoint, it has been estimated that there are about 60,000 qualified witches in the U.S.A. today, mostly operating on a non-coven basis. Anybody who believes in anything supernormal or supernatural with sufficient sincerity and intensity to convince others to believe the same, is on the royal road to witchcraft, with no stop-offs. That is how it happens in America and for a very good reason.

Witchcraft is closely associated with psychic phenomena; and where that field is concerned, America is the prime stamping ground. Indian legends are rich in ghostly lore and it was in their most powerful tribal territory — the Iroquois country of upper New York State — that modern spiritualism was born. There, two young girls, the Fox Sisters, somehow produced uncanny rappings that their parents took so seriously that they called in the neighbors, who were not just equally impressed, but more so. From that developed table tipping, the Ouija Board and finally the Duke University experiments in extra sensory perception, largely American innovations.

So it is not surprising that people should gather in Manhattan penthouses, suburban homesteads, or Greenwich Village pads and get so fired up by anything from ESP to LSD, that they begin receiving messages or gaining glimpses of the future. It's certainly more fun than gathering herbs, jumping over cauldrons, and waving sacrificial knives called "athanes" while chanting "Blessed be!" to prove that you don't intend to use them. It's more sophisticated, too.

When people gather for a social evening and begin to talk about ESP, somebody is almost sure to say, "If I had only brought my Ouija Board . . ." Upon hearing that, the hostess either brings out her own, or calls her next door neighbor and finds that she has one and asks her to bring it over and join the hexfest. Meanwhile, somebody is sure to pull out a tarot pack and start dealing and reading it for anybody who is interested. Always, a neglected guest can go into a corner and start pushing pins in his favorite voodoo doll, perhaps intending them for the very person who ignored him. So if people pass out at the party, don't be surprised, even though none of those already mentioned may be to blame.

You never can tell what color candles may be burning in the cellar, or what sort of talisman some guest may be wearing, or whether the drinks have been spiked with some potent potion to stimulate love or luck. Such items and many, many more are supplied by dealers who stock the implements of hexcraft and provide "do it yourself" instructions with every order. Gauged by that ever-expanding market, the figure of 60,000 American witches might well be set at 600,000; or even at 6,000,000, if all persons who might like to try it are included.

Many psychic parties, in contrast, are reminiscent of old-time spirit seances, but on a more modern scale. Nobody would be surprised if a tipping table happened to levitate itself in the midst of the surrounding sitters. In these days of lunar landings, weightlessness has become a scientific fact; not an occult phenomenon. With reincarnation becoming a popular belief, a Ouija message may simply be your own self talking back from somewhere in the past or future, rather than that of some disembodied spirit dwelling in some happy but implausible perpetual "Summerland."

Witch cults apparently are thriving in Southern California, partially because of its proximity to Mexico, where witchcraft has always been the rage. But the Southern California groups have been too busy with their own affairs to take cognizance of the commonweal, as all good witches should. Unlike the British Wicca, who for centuries have consistently raised tempests to repel invaders from their shores, all the Southern California covens together have been unable to dispel the smog perpetually hovering over Los Angeles, even though that city has its own official witch.

It could be that white witchery is on the way out, where California is concerned, for there a much more virulent phase of the craft has raised its dark and ugly head: Satanism. The spearhead of the expanding movement is a Church of Satan that holds a mock religious service with a nude model as a living altar in a roomy old manse replete with skeletons, tombstones and murals representing fiery scenes from hell. The presiding "high priest" of this conglomeration is a former carnival worker who has issued a Satanic Bible, with chapter introductions inscribed in a cryptic language termed "Enochian" which shows traces of various classical tongues, including Pig Latin.

Boldly, blatantly, this volume prescribes the Nine Satanic Statements, announces the advent of a new Satanic Age, lists the four Crown Princes of Hell: Satan, Lucifer, Belial, Leviathan; and follows with more than seventy Infernal Names, all helpful toward raising hell on earth. But when it comes to human sacrifice, the black book goes in for whitewash. Satanists, it would seem, could never countenance such a thing.

But it was countenanced in Paris in 1680, when a sorceress known as La Voisin provided great ladies with a "love powder" composed of the bones of toads, the teeth of moles, cantharides, iron filings, human blood and human dust. If that couldn't woo a lover from a rival's embraces, La Voisin furnished a more powerful mixture of secret ingredients that would dispose of the rival personally and permanently. This was politely termed an "inheritance powder," because it could also be used to shorten the remaining days of wealthy, elderly relatives.

To condition the noble clients to their parts as poisoners and insure their silence as well, they were initiated into the Black Mass by the renegade Abbé Guibourg, who followed the pattern that Satanists use today, even invoking the twin devils of lust, Astaroth and Asmodeus, whose names are still on the current list. But to render the ritual effective, the blood and ashes of an unbaptized infant were required, for which eager clients knowingly and willingly paid the price. When the *Affaire des Poisons*, as it came to be known, was finally brought to light and subjected to exhaustive investigation, it was estimated that La Voisin had disposed of more than 2,500 unwanted infants, though it was not stipulated how many were used for sacrificial purposes.

All this happened after witchcraft persecutions had all but run their course in France, so although the cases came under that head, they were actually a matter for criminal procedure, conducted by a special commission appointed by Louis XIV. Many of the charges against noble ladies were dropped, however, when it turned out that the king's mistress, Madame de Montespan, was deeply involved in the Satanic ceremonies and had even plotted against His Majesty's life. So much of the evidence was suppressed to avoid a court scandal.

The subsequent history of Satanism can be traced at recurrent intervals ever since, and it has left an unsavory heritage in its wake. Its recent revival may indeed be innocuous in itself, if kept within the confines of what may be its one and only "church." But according to reports, it has been spreading to the hinterlands; and it is a significant fact that the leader of a blood cult charged with mass murder and mayhem was practically worshipped as "Satan" by his obedient but deluded followers.